RESONATE
Aarav Chopra

AARAV CHOPRA

Copyright © 2021
Aarav Chopra
"Resonate"

All rights reserved. No part of this publication may be reproduced, distributed or conveyed without the permission of the author.

Cover Design/Interior Design: Mitch Green
radpublishing.co

RESONATE

In loving memory of
Jaskirat "Jasz" Singh Sandhu
Nov. 17th, 1996 – March 23rd, 2019

Sending voicemails to an angel,
Writing mixed letters over to God.
Pleading for Him to send back the soul we loved, until then we will hold our applause.

We all wish that we had some more time just to say, we loved you and your soul.
For wherever God has taken you...
Please remember -
That you made many feel so whole.

How you would lift us up so swiftly, individually, telling us everything we can do. Not for awhile, I doubt in our own lifetime will we savor a future without you.

Oh brother where have you gone, where have you gone now leaving us alone. Please come back to us, for like me there's many who will never get to know... Another soul like you will not return and our hearts will remain blue.
As we wish for you to breathe again, we all feel selfish that we do.

How we feel connected to your laughter, a memory that won't fade. How you healed each of our differences, tirelessly molding us all back to shape. You never ran away from our troubles, you were always there to save the day.

As we search for you dear brother...
We see many stars in the sky.
Even as they shoot, they don't quantify -
For your being sparked them in each of our eyes.

The orchestra that you were alone -
The voice inside your soul.
Will resonate with us forever,
There's no meaning of love you didn't show.

RESONATE

As we pray for your soul in Heaven, we wish it offers everything you need. For there are many on this Earth...oh so many hearts you touched close.
We would offer the air we breathe -
Just to send your life back home.

We love you dear brother, come back to us with your glow.
Never will I see a man, take care of as many heart's like you.
There will never be a melody, Jasz - there will never be another like you.

Fly your wings around each heart you touched, for we will never stop praying for you. Rest peacefully with the others, that God sent away too soon.

Teri yaad mein, Jasz

For Nikhil Choudhary, I am continuously thankful for your support. My motor never stops running, here I speak of a motor to be my mind. Not on your careful watch does it stop. Knowing that I am not an easy person to understand, yet you do and never fail to stand by my side through it all. You've fed me, you've clothed me, you've taken me to places my own two feet could not travel to. In the decade that we've known each other, you have filled my empty moments with more boost. The pressure only gets us out of the tunnel and into the sunlight again. We roar through it all, together.

What do you get when your depression finally meets your anxiety?

This book.

I have walked into many secure locations.
Read no weapons were allowed.
Yet, they let my mind in.
My words, are ammunition.
Prepare to be taken away from your seat,
and up to thought.
Hoping you relive these words,
Before any dangerous plot.
You are not your sadness.
Welcome to my madness.

AARAV CHOPRA

	Contents
R	Foreword by Sherri Dunn
E	In Your Eyes
S	(I Forgot Where This Was Going)
O	Wake Up
N	Nowhere, Somewhere
A	
T	
E	Thank You

Foreword by Sherri Dunn

Women aren't born into this world automatically programmed to become mothers. Some women make it easier than others and some women struggle with losing themselves in motherhood. Those women that make it seem easier, most of the time, have a tribe behind them that backs them up. The other women that struggle and tend to lose themselves, seeming to feel alone in their journey, don't always have the support groups in place. I know that motherhood isn't so black and white and there are many gray areas. What can be simple for one woman may seem like a defeat for another.

When I was a young girl, I never yearned to be a mother like some of the girls I knew. I was very worried I wouldn't be a good one and didn't want to take on such a huge responsibility in raising another human being. I took it very seriously and until my sister had children of her own; was I able to see the elation and the joyful wonders in motherhood; did I seriously consider having kids of my own. Her happiness around her children and the unconditional love that came with it was something to behold. I am so happy I gave motherhood a try because it made me the person I am today. It brought out the best sides of me in so many ways and I adore my children. I see the best parts of myself in them and I am so thankful to be their mother.

They are a truly glorious gift in my life. I wouldn't change my experiences for anything in the world. I strongly believe I was put on this Earth to be their mother. I did, however, have some very difficult times during my pregnancies and after my babies were born. I had Hyperemesis Gravidarum during both pregnancies and this made me extremely nauseous, dehydrated, and weak. I had a permanent port put into my arm so I could administer myself anti nausea medication at home. I lost so much weight during my first two trimesters that I looked ill, not pregnant. I had to get constant fluids into my body intravenously and to rest as much as I could. Strong smells would make me feel queasy, so

I avoided public places. I isolated myself out of necessity because being at home made it easier. I was fatigued to the point of exhaustion and felt very hopeless. No one forewarned me that this may happen and when I was suffering through it, I felt very alone. I sometimes think this may be the origin of my depression. The isolation I felt was unlike anything I'd ever experienced in my life. Once I had birthed both of my babies and the pregnancy hormones were out of my body, I felt back to myself again. The depression, however, seemed to stick to my bones. I was diagnosed with Post-Partum Depression after my first child and suffered in silence like so many women do because they feel ashamed.

Every human experience is unique. Everyone has the right to express those experiences in ways that give them some sense of relief. For me, that has always been writing poetry. When I am writing, I feel free to express myself and it gives me reprieve. My fondest memory of poetry and my first introduction to it was because of my Grandma Jeanne. She would write me poems and send them to me in the mail. I would eagerly write her back awaiting the next poems arrival. Her words and the way they were playfully placed on the page always made me smile and feel good inside. They came directly from her heart and they touched me deeply. It's as if she were right there beside me, whispering them into my my ear. I could hear her sweet voice whenever I read her words. The poems would transport me to where she was, and they brought me so much comfort.

Over the years I've had to find ways to deal with my depression, it is a part of me. There are moments in time where I find myself staring off into nothingness. Sometimes I don't even realize I've lost track of time until something snaps me back into reality. I yearn for days where I feel whole, where I feel more grounded both physically and mentally. I'm not ashamed to share my deepest sadness because I know there are others that feel the

same way. I want others to know they're not alone. I know so many of us share these dark spaces in time where we feel hopeless and damaged. I'm not identified by my sadness, I do have wonderful days often. I have so many blessings in my life and am thankful for my family and friends. I refuse to let depression shape me
but it's a daily struggle to keep the darkness away. When it knocks on my door, I have no choice but to let it in. My hope for you all is to be moved by the words in this book. Try and let the words fill your soul and sit with them for a while. There are truths to be told even though they may be hard to read. We are all searching for answers and the best we can do is share our experiences thus connecting us to others. I hope you find some sort of comfort knowing you are not alone in this world.

I believe the author of this book came into my life for a reason and it was to teach me how to love writing again. When he showed his vulnerability, I wanted to show mine. He was a pivotal person on my timeline. I haven't always taken the easiest road but in retrospect it's been a blessing. I've failed so many times over the course of my life and every time I learn something new about myself. The uncomfortable feelings I get when I struggle, force me up out of that dark space. No matter how dark my mind can get, I'm able to persevere because of the friendships that surround me. His is a true friendship I know I can always count on. He has become a part of my life and I'll forever be grateful. Our belief in each other lifts me up. I hope you can resonate with the ideas and thoughts in this book. I hope you feel some sense of relief. new about myself. The uncomfortable feelings I get when I struggle, force me up out of that dark space. No matter how dark my mind can get, I'm able to persevere because of the friendships that surround me. His is a true friendship I know I can always count on. He has become a part of my life and I'll forever be grateful. Our belief in each other lifts me up. I hope you can resonate with the ideas and thoughts in this book. I hope you feel some sense of relief.

AARAV CHOPRA

In

YOUR

Eyes

RESONATE

Greener pastures lie ahead, for you and I.
Evergreen memories, something only peace can wrap a bow
around till we die.
No matter where I go, there will be your eyes.
Together I feel ethereal, away I feel empowered.
Recall the ways you see me, the worth I feel inside.
You've sent these blessings to me, and I vow to live each moment
with you resonating in
my mind.

May I keep you here,
Where no one will see your grave.
Demons haunting my days, have they come to harvest this day from my shoulders.
I feel their control, I know.
They're deep in my own soul, how they growl and they grow.
In emptiness we fold,
Through kindness we can change their rustic molds.
May I raise you from here,
I wish for you to leave from my space.
Do you care about the damage I can't replace.
Oh demon, hello demon.
You're not walking over me today.
Oh demon, you poor demon.
My smile never changed since yesterday.
Welcome to your grave, I've been digging.
Welcome to your place, I have my own reasons.
Like resin on fine art you're damaging only those who wish for perfection.
I'm not your kind of perfect, believe me.
I'm not your kind of angel, believe me.
I've been carrying old souls with me through every season.
I'm a reaper of all my old demons.
I feel their control, oh I feel their control.
I don't know their names anymore, they've shifted faces.
Yet their energies are the same and I'm not complaining.
Everyone told me they could walk around me adjacent.
I'm truthfully in love with my angels,
I'm truthfully in love with my demons.
Hello maker, of this universe hello preacher.
How can I confess the bodies I've left in the trees as I plant them.
I only wish for them to grow in front of me.
New life something they will believe.
Every demon.
Every season.
Everyone was sent packing by me.

RESONATE

Don't you see.
May I show you to your grave, no worries my dear friends I'm okay.
I'm hopeful through all of the pain.
I'm still killing them, I'm still living man.
It's what everyone says I should do.
Yet where does it all start for you.
Do you just pray for it all to go away?
Your clean hands won't remove them, they can only ward them off.
So kill them off.
Roll up your sleeves,
Soil away your pain to let it all grow.
In a forest return to the fog, oh amoré
oh amoré.
I love how I rise,
and
.
.
.
they
.
.
.
.
fall.

My life consists of achievements I've yet to reach,
It consists of a unique sense of empathy I give -
I had to learn to not preach.
With the hollow passerby's that I let walk away,
What could my words give them, their demons are stalking them as I speak.
I won't consider them projects.
I pray that you don't as well.
Feel something real, offer something for them to feel.
For words no longer shift their senses,
If only a smile makes their day.
Pass one their way.

You begin to make a difference when you're there for a solution not simply hearing about their pain.

I say this to offer dual purpose, at times they've done what they could to reach out. They've talked to themselves about the exact situation that is difficult. At times, we must be aware that the release of their dark shares in life, requires a response that is beyond listening. I love that you have allowed yourself to listen as often as you have in life. Please believe that we, all humans can heal. We all have the ability to distract.

I pray that when another reaches out to you, you see a solution for them. For you are not in their tunnel. You only hear their echoes from outside.

You deeply feel the pain yourself when you feel locked.

Have they not been there for you before? Has a soul not reached out before? Somebody is out there. Dial the number. Send the message. Check on all your people. Strong ones, quiet ones. Distant ones. Learn their way of speech and come to them with a warm greeting.

It's not just listening that helped you, a stroll around town did. Endlessly ranting to another soul did. Watching a movie did. Sending a meme that made you laugh that day did. Chatting on camera did.

Please do more than just listen, remember your bliss can be shared. Their pain was shared, they trusted you and showed you its door.

Make a difference, make their difference. Be the hand of God they needed in that moment.

AARAV CHOPRA

It's okay to stay the same,
They're futuristic -
I'm still wearing black.
It's become ritualistic.
I don't follow your trends,
Some roads lead the same way so I won't follow your bends.
I'll be here by myself, where I have found peace and my own meaning of wealth.
To release from the line and hear nothing new.
Aside from a being or two.
Don't play & forget where we came from.
Pay it forward remember some report on the world not you and me.
Keep the faith on the way home,
Something tells me that last week, was my best I suppose.
So you can move forward I wish to repeat, not recourse.

Heavy is the soul of a mind with deadweight energy,
Forever living in a lucid reality.
Perceptions enamoring the charms of scentless roses,
Countless calamities.
Harvesting negatives turning misfortunes into only seconds of useful energy.
Motivation is not a gift to you, if not harnessed for safe keeping.
Your freedoms are not fleeting if you sit down for the tragedies.
Meet your mind in your most uncomfortable spaces.
Through those channels you'll earn the energy to remain tenacious.
If you're sitting in between black and white thoughts,
Feel free to bring color, life was meant for you to paint not go down around the chalk.

We're apex predators out in the open,
Howling at the moon.
Scarred on our fur yet still here for the troops.
In packs we hunt for prey unknown to you,
We'll make peace with those who don't aim for our backs.
Stay near, far, or dangerously close upon our tracks.
We're headed for the mountainsides, pacing with grace.
Leaving no scent, if we do, show your face -
Let us know if you're to be hunted,
Or a friend of our mutual fate.

RESONATE

I've fallen from the skyscrapers,
A vigilante masked in a suit and tie.
Remembering how quickly their eyes would fall,
Two feet forward soldier, their doors won't open ...
Hmm.
Why not blow past them. Have them worry about the solder.
Empty out their minds, remove their lies.
Quickly replace their emotions with love, empathy what a war drug.
Flowers at the end of my weapon.
Art not war.
My prices are not inflated, my memories are sober some remind me of sedation.
They will for us to create, empty out your wallets please.
Keep raising the bar, our currency you can't source.
You can not source.
Stop worrying where it all comes from.
You will grow tired of certain things, you've let art live on.
Pages I can fill, yet my screen is limitless.
Ask about me...

IN SPIRIT

When we create, we leave a mark on our timeline.
When we inspire, we lead another on their path.
When we meet, we reconcile memories of the pain and the strength needed to finish the course.
For we never gathered another's spirit for nothing easy. Right?
If it's in you let it drive you to the end.
Love with the spirit of your favorite marker of love.
Lead with the spirit of your favorite leader.
Create with the spirit of your favorite creator.

Lights!

Rolling….

Action….

Ty enjoys silver bullets down his chest, don't worry for I'm only mentioning the beer. He has shells in hand, the pistol is still taped under the bar and he knows no signal - just war. I track eyes as people walk through, especially with the men tipping their hat one too many times - someone's lost their marker. I find myself peering through steins and listening to a crowd of men tell the world about their boss and how each of them has their story about whose next in line. Don't ya just love it when you're next to the 8 bros. of a company. Without fail you'll know when they're ordering more shots.

-

The catcalling begins soon after, they're all fuckin' someone in their mind right now. A few of them have wedding bands on, my cigarettes should burn their necks. They love gazing into souls who wish to know nothing of their breathe. They keep screaming what's on it anyway. "Bvartender! Vvmore Vodka!" My bourbon is now mostly ice and what a heinous crime that is.

-

I seek to leave the reckless men before one slips on his wingtips and breaks his jaw before I could plan on catching him. Maybe I envisioned that in a dream once, I just didn't want that to become a reality tonight. Besides either he falls or that brunette he's eyeing spills her rosé purposely but says it's an accident. Ty removes the pistol and followed me towards the alley and brings out an OG whatever ya wanna call it and we pass and go on about life.

-

We displayed our lung power for a few minutes, I could've sworn he rolled a gram that night. I don't know what I was thinking, that I could keep up with all 6'7 320lbs. of his lungs or the endless supply he tended to have on him. Loaded is how I definitely felt, I then looked to the back door where one of the office guys was tossed out followed by two more.

-

"Guess we dodged something, they play too much man. Let's bounce. Jax's is still open and ya know they got the specials tonight." Ty loved his top 40s with 40s in hand and his women with a hint of clothing. I was too blown to go into another place with recycled air and for some godforsaken reason I saw your name on a piece of litter. It can't be you for you're probably miles away but why did each letter match on that receipt, Starbucks so ordinary but the order was a Grande Americano. Just like yours...

-

"Man - the hell you doing?! Let's go they have this place on the verge of getting shut down. I'm trying to make things happen not get into another scrum. I just hit up Cooks he knows we're pulling up." I knew then Ty was not taking no for an answer and he just wanted to leave. I was cemented to the ground and I held onto that receipt for what seemed like forever.

-

Before it's too late I want to tell you I loved you.
For I'm departing now and I can't love you anymore.
There's a corner of this Earth that belongs to me and it was you who made this space my corner.
I once grew so tall in love the fairy tales of beanstalks would marvel at me. I had a warm soul before I exited through you, cold and unwavering. I'm not here to smile anymore, I once loved you. Summer ended, I found your heart matching leaves in October. Hopelessly losing your form from my branches you claimed your glories from. I found my home and as the key turned, the lock accepted me. The lock no longer protects you and I can still call this place home.

-

It was a new day, I felt cemented because I don't remember getting to Jax's. I opened my wallet to see how much trouble I got into last night and what I found was even worse. I took the receipt with me, it made its way into my home. By chance so did your name, albeit on paper I needed coffee so I'm now sitting at a Starbucks having a Grande Americano with my new receipt next to the one I found last night.

\-

Ty

Text Message -

"Man...remind me to never bring out that strain again my dude you were calling her name out all night long. I know fasho you had like four old fashions. You were mumbling in your sleep the minute I got to Jax's I flipped a light and tossed yo ass inside your house. I'm glad I did that because they got Cooks last night man. Some cats drove by and sprayed Jax's down good, whole blocks a mess I'm glad you fell asleep brudda. Hit me when you're up and let's make some moves."

\-

I could only think of one response for him, that I'm not done loving her and her name isn't done saving me.

CUT

Send her into the nightly mist,
Understand that it comforts her.
Shine the moonlight through her window, offer her a shooting star again.
Hinder her from nothing, let her be so she won't have to explain.
May her path be clean but the road not too simple.
In every land no matter how dark there's an angel,
Turning over every stone, remaining so humble and able.
Heartwarming and caring, one who offers clarity while others tell fables, oh she's nothing
this world has seen.
Astros, comets, galaxies, she's a dream.

FEARFUL

I fear where you are and where you will go,
You see what you are is everything I'd ever wanted.
Could be fools gold.
Bread before the mold.
You're not a thing, you're a being.
Someone of value, someone who deserves to bask in sunlight.
If you want we can laugh, we can smile, or we can even cry.
I fear what you will become-
Don't jump, just come home.

RESONATE

My mind is a trigger finger,
You've been in the way.
I must move past you to earn my honest pay.
Momma needs her meds and you no longer have a say.
You've stopped calling here, you've run away.
You've stopped living here, why are you praying so much I ask still to this day.
How many times have I spited my fathers in my head for taking away my name.
I am my own man, I've healed to the point to say:
Let the spirits and lord provide for you,
The memory of you leaving first.
On your judgment day.
"Sorry little boy, stupid little dreams."
I'm a man now, don't come near my family.

I've stumbled in many ways just as I've been sent to the ground a few.
Felt many ways about it.
As they called me names, I learned how to argue and what an argument does to me.
I studied their speech, where they found fun I found spite.
Causing me to fall in many other ways forgetting what my childhood was meant to be -
Trying to be a grown up.
Standing tall today, writing down what they use to stay.
Black boy on the black top.
Hearing the same wrong stories out of their lips.
Brown boy go take a bath you smell like your lunch.
You can't play here, don't you have a tutor to go to?
See - you're just not fit. You just have a different way of being American - so does that
make me counterfeit?
I crossed my heart and sang the anthem, side by side.
Here I stand through all of it.
Some of them are parents now, some of them I still see.
I have a stronger mind to speak now, back then I let it all get to me.

RESONATE

Bring me your energy, bring me your pain.
Sunshine or rain, tell me you are one against the grain.
I wish to not see a soul leave your body.
The test of time fixated on all of its turmoil.
I will stand on your pedestal –
Right next to you.
For I am an equal –
Whether we discriminate a red against a blue.
How we judge the color of ties in the rooms, versus shirts in the streets.
Tell me we're able to walk on our own two feet, lest abilities taken from us where they
ask of us to not practice our speech.

REGARDLESS

I've asked of people, their name and their favorite places.
I've heard some say my favorites back, I no longer remember their faces.
I've met more than a thousand human beings,
By name I can share their stories.
I must learn to remember their faces.

RESONATE

Gravitate towards the center,
I never came to believe.
Meditate away from the travesties.
How can you escape a mind, breathing atrocities.
When cities scream and hedonists sing.
Who will detach me from this nightmarish dream.
I will not rest my eyes on this chapter.
Till the one with the trigger, says I actually matter.
Emulate my sorrow, please take your time.
I've seen clouds...where they don't belong.
Same old song, same old song, same old song.
Are we living to recourse their thrills.
Unabridged villains.
Smile for me demons, treason looks good only on you.

Anger to me is a passive emotion that is suppressed by a deeply layered learning curve. There are many aspects of anger and you can argue there are stages of it as well but for today, I want to focus on self-deprecation. Whenever we put ourselves down, we're angry with ourselves for what? An unfortunate example is when we let go of a habit or a person we once found happiness with. It's easy to blame yourself, it's easy to tell yourself stories when you felt less valued by the people around you. Especially when you can see physical or emotional changes in you from not being you for awhile even simply a day.

Today, remember that you're allowed to learn yourself. Forgive yourself. Be yourself. Nothing you've done, fails the version of you 5 years ago. Give yourself the credit you deserve today.

RESONATE

A reckoning will find you, parking near your doorstep.
Lingering alongside the surface edges of your tables.
Dusted like your memories of a new hope.
Trepidations take you apart,
From the lub dubs your heart was too frozen to feel.
As if the seizing breathes, heard no blessings from another.
This pain you feel alone.
This renovation of your soul -
Was tasked to your zones.
The many you have.
In your mind -
Trying to find it all,
Is a being ever fully grown?

Soon they say, we'll have it all to replace what didn't work before.
Under what sun will we leave for that mirage.
Serenity I will not trade for sabotage.
How are we to forget what made us who we are?
Must we let robots do now what man did to set and raise the bar.
Invent to renew or replenish but please don't limit our race -
Think about our sustenance.
How we're surrounded by many recycled architectural bits.
Awaken please acknowledge this, how are we so forward thinking yet behind on nostalgic bliss.

Depressants bring me down, double shots in my glass.
Outlets for my pain, smoke sticks to my veins. I'm clinically insane over what I can't contain -
I seek answers from the mundane.
Yet...
I'm over it all, I'm tossing the bottle. I've finished the drops, a teary red eyed demon.
I'm living full throttle, how much energy was lost.
I feel better when I'm not thinking of my sickness, I've written out many of my own prescriptions.
At times I feel alone, it's best to -
My decision.
Down the hatch, another liquid.
Maybe it's clear, maybe it's viscous.
Tennessee Honey or tap water as it glistens.
I'm an addict of self affliction,
I overthink my every decision.
I see myself follow more than I break traditions.
To those that want the failure of my life,
I'll overcome more than I listen to the pain you wish I submit to.
I am not falling anymore, I may look down at the concrete.
To thank the men and women who laid it,
but I'll look up to see these eyes of my mine.
In mirrors I stand tall, only they're so tilted.
I'm proud of my life, my reason for wanting everything, has shifted.
I just want to be me.
Sobriety.

Let there be whispers from Eden,
Of places with prose and poetry.
Kept distant from people with no charm,
In the many places they wish to leave us.
As if our words don't belong.
There is no combination to freedom,
That I haven't changed to save myself.
In broken choruses and rhymes,
I beg forgiveness to the readers of my story.
When the skyline matches the night,
Colorful yet not so bright.
In hidden corners I remain,
A man with many words -
Speaking in stanzas, not tongues.
So do you question my Lord's name.
Or wish to know,
which Lord takes place
in a poet's brain.

Unlearning
The more of you I learn,
The more of you I forget.
I felt more of you before,
Now I'm told to neglect.
I've understood so many patterns before,
Now all I must do is hear your echoes.
I no longer feel the world outside.
Least I can say for the days I stay inside.

I've loaded a pistol before, shot at targets.
Felt the cold weight of bullets, watched as they pierce through paper so I won't have to imagine what they'd do to a door.
Thanks television.
Law & Order.
Who is on the other side.
A wall to collect the shells.
I'm walking on marble floors.
Heists on my mind.
Sweet mouth my way into vaults, you've been slipped of your keys.
That's not my fault.
Only my doing.
Highway robberies are too expensive.
Don't let me through, I'll take your time.
Leave you mystified.
In a flash of a second, you've given me the next set of moves.
Your cameras witnessed my spells, the many souls I've consumed.
In and out.
Contract complete.
Wondering how this revolver still has every bullet left, what a treat.

Why do you question the way I care about myself more than you? Finding the meaning of my soul is better than hearing my own say, "I do." I'm as quiet as the captions on your screen.
Gestures can get me by in this life -
Only water makes a sound against this body as I cleanse what's apart of me. I can smile without your permission, your adoration does not appease me.
As I grew into these shoes, my feet began to rest -
For they no longer grow, yet here come all the miles...
Flights of stairs, branches on these trails - as if it were all a test.
I am not freed by another man, I have my own acts to see through,
Don't love me for what you see, you won't get through my chest.
My mind is not hollow, my pride is mine to keep.
Each moment you try to separate me from myself, it's only beloved gravity that begs of me.
To stay grounded and one with the soul I was given,
Here forever, here forever -
So far I have seen.
Destruction of myself and reparations.
How resilient I have been.
My mind brings me peace -
So don't worry about my happiness.
I'm a burning candle with no end,
I'll burn like the core of this Earth.
Unaccessible to no man, I am peacefully centered.
My life needs no witness, away from the energy of those who created me.
If you're here to offer boundaries, I'll protect myself and my family.
I am not dependent on anyone, if my own blood already welcomes me.
Softly going over each detail, adding words to emote gray when needed - I can't see myself erasing thoughts about you. Your eyes, I wish for their direction, please let me read your emotions as you skip out on the words.
Come to me like a spray can, tag along my journey. Let's run to where they won't and lay claim to what we find. For isn't that how it was once before? Have they stopped seeking with their eyes, a uniform was once about clothes - now we're surrounded by ideas.

I am leaving this world on a day to day basis but there's a "forever" the people of this world speak of.
Maker don't take me yet. I care for only her eyes, I am not ready to see them fold before me. For as hers fold, my mind will be erased. Each part of her story won't be new, and all I will have left is to trace.
You never welcomed yourself near a place of love in a while and neither have I.
What's painfully clear, is how we both wish to disappear.
Not to each other but from this ungodly fear -
Of a God to believe in, or finding an honest person to wish faith into our ear.
Upon hearing their stories, I question why their tales turned to splits.
I'm upset with this world and some of its lovers who just drop their gifts.
Turntables will teach you to follow the order,
There's a process if you wish to hear your tunes.
I've yet to hear of a man placing the needle right where he wished to, if not starting
from the top.
How advanced we are now.
A steady stream of consciousness is no longer common.
If one speaks his mind, he is sent to love himself -
On a lonely island.

Those furthest from the way you live feel attached to you. It's futile for them to lead their life based on your energy. You're doing yourself a favor by letting them watch and not lead.

I want to smile with my heart, so lead my body through the fog so I can be the one with the mist.
Read Rosangela to me, mix the tea leaves with cardamom -
Rewind the cassettes before we go.
Bring only one key when we leave -
For I have my faith in you,
Script me down the paths you choose.
Send me down the streets that have felt you.
Not in a way I can feel, but offer me the deliverance of a new world.
Spoil no bend in this journey, run your fingers through my hands at stoplights.
Tell me about the time you had your hair in curls.
I could live in this world blindfolded, for everyday feels bright -
In a world of darkness, I'll have you as my girl.

RESONATE

Through empty nights and no love,
I've forgotten how companionship tastes on my lips.
For the next person I touch will love me like a virgin.
For I've been afraid for so long, as I've heard the journeys others go through.
I've seen people quietly mold themselves into likable beings,
Have they held onto the meaning of my name before they wish to make me sing?
I'm so removed from the choruses of heartstrings, no living being can send life back into me in one night.
I don't need a bed to make peace, my mind has become my home.
If you're here to love me, tell my nerves you're here to stay.
I cannot let you near me, if I can't savor you from afar.
I may want what's rare, I find so much more behind ones eyes -
One day I'll remember belonging, and it won't always be like this.
The patience I have now, will speak volumes to the next person I choose to lay with.

I've stumbled in many ways just as I've been sent to the ground a few.
Felt many ways about it,
As they called me names, I learned how to argue and what an argument does to me.
I studied their speech,
Where they found fun
I found spite.
Causing me then to fall in many other ways
Forgetting what my childhood was meant to be -
Trying to be a grown up.
Standing tall today, writing down what they use to stay.
Black boy on the black top.
Hearing the same wrong stories out of their lips.
Brown boy go take a bath you smell like your lunch.
You can't play here, don't you have a tutor to go to?
See - you're just not fit. You just have a different way of being American -
Does that make me counterfeit?
Here I stand, I rise, I sing through all of it.
Some of them are parents now, some of them I still see.
I have a stronger mind to speak now, back then I let it all get to me.

Do I see many honest paths, or am I too acquainted with hope.
Do I see fountains of youth and brilliance in everyone,
Am I searching for certain things?
Have I become a type of person to be specified,
Do I requisition myself to certain causes without knowing all of the hidden lies.
I don't wish for things to end, yet I'm here when they sever.
I'm here as they sever.
Honest paths lead somewhere...
I know I'm not the only one out there -
To see the reverse then left with despair.
What we learn shouldn't change how we care.
Not all paths lead to the guilty in our nightmares.

Here we are harvesting away, giving ourselves away with the hope to grow. Equal paths aren't found in this life, with each step someone's bound to leave. Just keep following your path, it's yours to know.

I've pitted your lies and they aren't as bitter as olives.
They're not as pure like the branches held in greek theatre, no.
I was never made aware that I'd fall victim to an audition.
For no hopeful lover will I sin, be sure of what you want with me.
Draw me closer, my scent is one you haven't had before.
Tell me as many truths about me in succession, my minimum expectation is for you to impress me.
May hell freeze over if you have forgotten my name.
Spare me what's scripted, in private share your lines.
I haven't experienced as many bodies as you, not the way you're requesting of me.
When you open your door to the world, take note of the wind.
How it lets you go, unlike the problems left in your home.
Be mindful, for if another's presence offers direction to you where are you headed?
Don't dress me as the dead, to leave me feeling awakened.

As the world gets colder, you shouldn't. I hope you realize how much time you have had given back to you. How others went more than beyond their way throughout the years to care. Contact itself would help us. A simple hug would take many worries away.

Do you recall your last unhappy moment? Who pulled you out of that. Did you return when you were centered to thank them, did you stop to think how they are. It becomes a hard life for us all eventually. Continue to check on each other, as much as you do yourself.

I've spent December's alone, they ruin your January's. Change someone's mind about how they move forward today in their life. Create a habit of helping where you can and you'll enrich every environment you walk into.

There aren't many that live like this,
Alone - leaving their marks from a distance.
Conscious of the lands away from home that pose a threat.
You'll need more than strategy to track me, these wins don't offer me trophies.
Only what is needed to carry onwards.
The countless sprints up mountainous paths,
Helped channel the spirit of a full moon in these bones.
Tell all my prey that I have a family,
Alter any resolution in their head where they wish to see me go quietly.
These eyes light the night differently,
Hidden in a borealis is every prayer I've sent away.
I will chase these demons, tell my angels to watch for me.
One by one missing not a single midnight, spare me no oversight.
This is my purpose, I will howl to protect what I have in sight.

I'm not tired of your negativity I just left from there.
Remember me as the person who did care -
But after I realized how you loved your burdens I decided to leave you in that air.
There's only so much I can do.
There's only so much I can say.
Forgetting it all is not my choice, helping you understand it all till it's okay.
Don't look at me as medicine -
I'm not in a cabinet for your needs.
Not prescribed by your doctor,
Your thoughts matter but won't make me bleed.
So I promise you, I'm not tired of your negativity -
You've done so much to let it breathe.
Just remember this goodbye as the last time you'll hear from me.

The day I knew I loved you was the day everything changed.
Every second on the hour that I was away began the meter.
Like it wasn't fair to be away from you yet the, "I miss you's,"
started from the first step away.
My heartbeat would rhythm to the sound of, "I do."
My eyes if they weren't set onto your color of hues, I would blink
and every time they did, they were gesturing that I love you.
My arms would reach for the tangible things in life but then I'd
think of where I'd leave my hands while I love you.
Each step towards you was safer and I knew I was getting where
I've always wanted to.
Politely I'd go about my day forgetting others voices while
playing their sentences back with the sound of you.
How your sweet gentle tones would arouse my soul,
How deafening your pleasures would sound as we made each
other feel whole.
It's you that keeps my heart alive and you that makes me pure.
I love that I've waited for you, a woman I was meant to love
fearlessly as my cure.
The day I knew I loved you, I began to prepare for whatever else
I need to endure.
Just to love you.

RESONATE

We're planets awaiting discovery and the stars have begun to run far away from us.
I fear you're polluting your mind like they did our Earth.
I am conscious and considerate, sober to your belligerence.
God was called on one too many times and here we are repenting to him.
He may have heard us say, "fuck this," one too many times.
The hours of effort and the tears that were spent.
On all sides of the Earth I'll continue to pray that the lights stay on,
On my side of the Earth I'll question where do I belong.
And if I must belong there -
Who will discover the planet in me.
The ability to create and foster a new reality.
Open this door I am not here to run.
For every moment they harmed me,
You offered me purpose and I'm not here to frown at the sight of a gun.
For if they wish to end a life worth living,
I'll accept a bullet to leave them with regret.
I haven't met my maker, I say His name with grace.
I'm not here to change - any part of my fate.

I used to hate it and had to love it,
Knew about it and still left it.
Cared for it all and forgot it.
Licked my wounds and solved it.
Without you or taking you along.
Jumping towards another...
home.

RESONATE

In between your breathes as you finish your ask,
I'll catch my breath and say yes.
That's how it will be, with your energy.
Don't flutter too far from the ridge or begin to worry.
Risen with your love.
Was asking for your heart too much to agree to?
Anything after, is no longer a task.
Hide me between your chest,
You'll rest amongst my wings.
We'll fly to where it is safe.
Just remember from here, nothing is a command or an order.
So finish telling me your wishes, acceptance is no longer something you should ponder.
Actions louder than the "I love you," traditions.

I cannot accept men seeding in multiple gardens and never
wanting to stay in the soil that will grow their roots the most.
To be so daring and unequivocally rude to every host.
If that's what they see you as, leave.
Let yourself become distant, when they request to hold you close.
He who charms one, greed leads him to charm many.
She who turns down one, is bothered by plenty.
The garden boy, the tool man.
-
As a man I stand in the shadows of the others,
Well aware of their poison -
Foolishly considering me a brother.
Women tell me what our men have done,
It's something I have to live for.
To speak against the tarnished ones.
Once bitter, no additive will make him sweet.
You'll never have her lips, romancing her in the heat.
For you've left to water homes that weren't yours,
Promising to build where the doors are now closed.
-
A man building his hell, doesn't deserve to live within the heaven
found in you.

I advance it all to be this painful at times.
Everything scars, scabs, or leaves marks and we still try to figure out if Mars can be had.
When will this millennium meet the proper course...
Can anyone -
Commit.
Follow fake feelings destined towards real journeymen.
It's gut wrenching leaving you comatose.
Whose to wake you?
Everyone prays for a final host?
Right. At least I expect it all to be painful -
If they turnout unfaithful.
Looks can be dangerous but that's why I'm friends with snickering devil's.
Gather along...remember they once were some angels.
Redemption offers belonging -
Don't feed me forever,
I have grown tired of its offering.

Before it's too late, I wanted to tell you I loved you.
For I'm departing now and I can't love you anymore.
There's a corner of this Earth that belongs to me and it was you who made this space a corner.
I once grew so tall in love fairy tales of beanstalks would marvel at me. I had a warm soul before I exited through you cold and unwavering.
I'm not here to smile anymore, I once loved you.
Summer ended, I found your heart matching the grounded leaves in October.
Hopelessly losing your form from the branches you claimed your glories from.
I found my home and as the key turned the lock accepted me.
The lock no longer protects you.

RESONATE

My scars came from the many battles from those I love,
I requested their love and received only pain.
My ways were not aligned with their higher council,
Leaving fury as the only option left in my veins.
I've never been the one to preach my ways with those who showed no sense of belonging in my thoughts.
Rebellion is something that boils, so as you come to heal me remember what happens when you touch me like a pot.
Recall my ways of thinking, I've been abused by others and let them walk peacefully.
I've been mishandled by lovers and see that they still think of me.
For as long as I dream of harmony, Those who question my freedom I will not let go of silently.
You will hear me beat my chest, feel the scars on my face.
Till these enemies are no longer within trace.

Where I sleep isn't where I rest,
It isn't where I reward myself.
It's where my hearts content.
Wherever that is I may not know,
I can only speak to my demons in places in my head.
I feel wrong for typing these words and not telling a therapist instead.
So where I sleep may not be the real question?
It's where do my angels stop watching over me instead.
-
Twenty Eight

RESONATE

Questioning your mold, was never the path to manifestation.
Residing in your wishes for redos won't matter when you reach a certain age.
Muslim to Hindu, a journey of recognition, of my lineage.
Twenty eight, full plates.
10 years ago, it was keep up and be there.
Don't be late.
Time has slowed, doors have closed.
Thousands more I've opened with my voice.
Beauty chills, it stirs till you thaw out your own acceptance.
Your feature, your voice. Your mind, your heart.
A soul may turn old, yet the memories will continue to fold.
Into places you will know, your stories will have to be told.
You're no longer young, let that never be the case.
Forevermore hold your head, forevermore will you go forward.
Liquor no longer pleases you, only the heavens do you chase.
Hate never sits in your mind, you rid yourself of your ego.
Tough task, we know.
Humble thyself, you're forever young.
This earth is not a home for you, this gravity was only a test of your time.

Cherry colored eyes, sweet surprise.
A virgin love, confused thinking sex is a drug.
Skipping the love.
Forgetful of the damage - the stress the burdens.
An ellipses morning, in another bed.
...
Who did what to me and who was had?
Was it even magic was last night?
Were you pleasured or left to be sad.
Learn the love, first.
Painfully each exit hurts.
Online if you're swiping, are you living the values of your heart or thirsting with your eyes.
Cherry colored eyes, a sweet surprise.
Don't belittle your being to ruin another hearts love cries.

She never stayed the same for any man. I want her to continue that trend for as long as I know her. I found her beautiful and each day I find that she adds to it. I found her free and each day I find that she sets her own smile below her eyes. She's not the one for the stable. Normalcy escapes her the same way it does for me.
Her mind ruptures complacent hearts, it is too easy for her. She stares into your soul knowing you weren't prepared & not the one. I want her to change as the times go, ebb and flow with her ego. She's a camouflage I wish to hide away with in broad daylight - moving in silence like spirits. I don't want to be the change, I wish to be her only constant.

I've been trying to find love, it's been scarring, roughness in my skin.
Dried up realities a mushroom cloud is what I'm in.
Warped into the possibilities of defeat and sadness.
Never forgetting hope and forward progress.
Love is just another pill to digest.
24 hours once a day.
Remember to love yourself -
A daily reminder is needed.
For many not just you.
Double up, buckle up bundle up.
Two sides to your heart,
Only you are its seamstress.
Stitching together what you believe in won't get you far these days.
Have you been counted out,
Have you been found.
Heavy heavy hands painful memories return again.

RESONATE

I give up on love it no longer feels like a drug,
I've been trying to call every heart like their number was in my phone book.
Yet no one picks up when I call -
The logs say missed missed missed them all.
Hearts no longer make sense to me.
They only matter to me if I see my own in echocardiograms.
I give up on love, it's no longer a drug.
Blinded by it no longer.
Saved by my heart forever.
Moving on, from loving -
Moving into, loving...me.

Lights!

Rolling….

Action….

REFUGE

The door number was 13. The one with the cigarette sign burn spotted by my hands. Must've made you cry in fear of the rage held in me that night. The delayed reactions to early angst made you realize I wasn't out of line. You held me in good faith.
The outsiders looked at us as if were strangers. I deeply felt that way. You see I rolled my own cigarettes back home, I only picked up this as an American tradition. Yet my papers said that the American brew I drank was no longer meant for me. I am no other. I am only human. You threatened to kick out my family then begin to ask why I cannot stand still. I only envisioned this day to be different. My scars tell different stories tonight.

My ears heard chills of my family that will keep me up at night. I am a man who cannot defeat a letter. Not now at least. Pray for my family I tell you this all I can seek.

For no matter what I said they wouldn't let me across and sentenced us all to dwell back to our native seas. I've structured my life to belong in both places. The feelings I've gone through I'll never take back or ask them to be replaced with. Don't worry about their declaration letter, worry about what they've done to me. Classified as a political outcry rather than a human who can sit down with you and enjoy your rubbish tea. In anger I go on to say one man's freedom is his passed onto others. Protect them to earn me. This executive order granted me a hotel room, not my typical bed and usual bar with an array of global whiskey.

My family cannot play with their chandelier lights dimming them lower then brighter to shine their lights on me. You took it away. One stroke of a pen. This isn't over. I know your nation and its citizens will rebel to fight for my kind in the end.

After my ruthless denial of your meaning,
I find that I only want you.
I've disarmed my nature and accepted that you are what makes me whole.
It eats away at me.
How your eyes bring comfort,
Something a bystander will never understand.
How I can't fathom the thought of you with another man.
I just can't.
Denying what you mean is not my freedom.
I just cannot fight myself for who you are and now I've found many reasons.
And every reason tells me I want you.
So maybe I'm asking for a disaster,
Impending emotions I'm well aware -
Please don't feel the need to pastor.
I feel waves of energy, I've yet to explain myself.
Please remove all restraints, conversations I have in my head.
Judged by many and himself.
Here to see a better way out.
Right now I'm headed for a passage of love or a disaster.
There's many things out there I wish to master.
One is patience,
Another is grace.
I wish to do so much with you,
I shouldn't be here questioning our fate.

RESONATE

My mind is a favela,
True to its core with its fair share of love struck corruption.
Maybe the sober me likes what the separate side of me does.
Another part of my being, where the borders cross I twist choices with drifted anxiety.
My thoughts are infidels and my actions fight against them for domination.
I wage wars against expectations and hunt for justice through humble silence.
The streets are menacing and I'm here with my own violence.
My mind is a favela,
True to its core with its fair share of love struck corruption.

Your pain never found its way to me,
I wanted to take some on.
I looked for it.
I looked for you.
I lost you to pain.
To hell with it all...if I lose you to something I can't tame.
Was I unable to learn your source of will power,
Which I know by now isn't me.

RESONATE

As I began to love,
You baited me with a forever.
So I welcomed myself to where I was before.
Ready to serve a purpose that will deceive me.
For you made no space in your soul.
Am I following a hell stricken pattern -
Am I merely a dot to you?
I cannot connect to what you refuse to create,
Steady hands, I can't relate -
Give me a place to rest my heart as I wait.
I don't want to be the reason you fold your heart.
The one to blame for the things falling apart.
I can bare to hold the weight of your burdens.
If you offered me the return of my time, I wouldn't be deserted.
I've been hollowed out and cast away.
I no longer have love left for myself.
This feeling I know too well.

I never wish to release your name to others,
I keep you so safely in my mind.
There's a place for you in all of me, each part of you equally shines.
There is no meaning of you that is tainted by the remarks of others, I am leaving them without a clue.
For all they know is that I am in love, just so happens that it's with you.
The nameless figure they wish to know, my inner circle rejoices with my happiness and that's all credit to you.
I do not believe in pedestals, I do believe in secrecy.
I know how you choose to love,
Loud and sinfully.
I'd show you the world quietly,
Together we'd walk privately.
You are the mythical eighth wonder of this world, passports full.
Everyone else is wondering where my hearts headed -
Asking how a person could have such a gravitational pull?
They never found out,
And it will always be you.

1-800-799-SAFE
HELP REDUCE DV BY PROMOTING THIS NUMBER

Tell me why you're here...
Why did you choose to come back?
I've gone ahead and bettered myself - fixed all the things you said I lacked.
I believed you at some point in time.
Your word meant more to me than anyone else in mind.
I thought I was doing it to please you but truthfully it was never enough.
I smiled more, cared more, still did all the things you loved and watched you fall
asleep.
I put your demons to rest every night so you didn't wake up weak.
I let you do as you wished because it all made sense to me when you kissed my lips.
The pain has left from the images of you.
The sadness I kept faded away like the scent of you.
So I ask again, why are you here?
Simply because you were in the area and shed a couple tears?
I'm no longer yours - I'm here because I chose to protect.
The place that I call home, the sanctuary that you left.

RESONATE

I am not to be kept away for anger therapy.
I brought a child into this world with you, I did so happily.
Don't wage wars on heartstrings that can tune differently.
Relief sinks in after silencing the beatings in my head.
I will leave you to come back, my foolish heart doesn't surprise me.
The rumbling pain you would deal, knowing I didn't deserve to bleed.
Nor should the person to the left or right of me.
I was molded to fear your dominance and you're no longer what consumes me.
If I can strip you of your choices I will be free.
Terrifying is how my eyes see you to be -
This shelter will offer me the freedom amongst the anger you left marks for others to see.
This revival is sweeter than the nectar you want,
After so long water on my skin feels it's natural state.
No longer do I burn for you to come home,
To wash yesterday away -
Giving you a new canvas to create.
All your destruction and envy upon my being.
I can tell you I look beautiful in every dress now,
The scars are no longer interested in seeing you.
They're gone and I paint with my charisma
A persona you haven't seen.
But helped create -
A life I struggled through but I now call safe.

If you're to love a woman craft a kind of love outsiders would call a masterpiece.
You only get one heart as a canvas to work with. So don't make an art gallery of lovers you split time with. Make one woman your monument.

If you want to be the man they don't talk negatively about, do better than the men you hear about. I find it absolutely childish that men blame women for being jumpy when we know first hand what we are capable of. I can honestly say that I know how fear stricken women are nowadays for I've heard stories I'd never retell.
Behind their back so much can go on and even as they stand side by side their men, they can't control where their eyes go.
So fellas you can engage with her mind without making room for another. You can dine with her and forget your phone at home. You should treat her to hours of conversation and spend the time instead of your money. A bracelet will only get tossed away after you lie, if you are to offer her one at least remember the weight on a mind after you can no longer hold her wrist. Give her moments to smile in your memory. A reason to crave you at home.

After a day shared in the heat who would you want to come home to? Or would you rather stare at what is perfectly okay being beautiful alone without the need of your gaze. Lower yours.

RESONATE

I promise to you that my words will never cut you.
Softly they might leave impressions but I never wish for you to bleed. If there were to be a day where your blood drips I want that call,
I want to be there to stop it before it flushes out the feelings in you. Before it takes away the life I've protected.
I would never harm you.
I wish to heal you.
Turn your spirit to mine,
Please allow me to love and heal you,
Time after time after time.

I want closure before you take silence as my final answer. Our hearts love tests, I only wish to take this one myself. Remember I don't need you, so let me howl at the moon till you no longer blind me from the sun. I think it's best you listen to me and decide now is not the time to run. Times up.
Put your paper heart down. The ink in your pen doesn't know you lie.

Look at the reaper you created, the person you once loved. The man who once smiled with you, caught your tears, wiped the blood. All of the above and of course we once had something we called love. A love that mattered, a love that made us care. Now look at us...is any of this fair?

"Fair," is only a term two parties use to barter luck.

When did I become brittle and young again? They begin to harm you past 25 and the words begin to stick. I have carelessly lost things that should matter more to me.
I remember those who left when I needed them most. Waiting for them to cut their distance and welcome me back near their breathe. Just to tell them they're nothing to bet on anymore. I'll bet on myself.

RESONATE

Lately even my words have been selfish,
I'm after things I can't go without waiting for.
I can't help it.
There are results from old tests no one speaks about.
Sadness I've rooted in me, can't free without the dealers help.
Hope I've left in others wondering if it's been used for anybody else.
On the surface you'll see a man whose willing to listen more than be heard.
Under a microscope you'll see these words.

I want to lover her in layers,
Peel back the moments of the naysayers.
See her in chapters,
Read her story.
Become a part of the story, there till the final chapter.
Every layer,
Every chapter.

RESONATE

I'll take care of things you told me,
Even as you're away.
The plants still need water,
The house needs to be dusted.
I have to fill my heart again,
The one who did before can no longer be trusted.

As the world crumbles without lasting honesty,
We wonder if any are leftover with bones of truth.
Our closets are full of masks worn to disguise the nightmares we live in.
I'll tackle the world in black when I wish to be as silent as my hope that day.
I'll show them a loud red, one day to let them know they can't silence me forever.
I'll walk the line in white to be the color of the bones that others find no truth in.
Only to remind the world that I'm as colorful as my dreams,
As vivid as my foresight -
Deflecting the lies the sinner tries to protect.

RESONATE

Be there for the fire or the flood.
When they're angry or in tears.
Even if they act like hurricanes -
You shouldn't disappear

You're now a touchy subject,
A shade of yellow that brings caution -
With peril stricken eyes.
A mind left with only selfish options.
The divider in the road marked with damage from before.
You've always marveled after blades,
You're now so sharp -
You're begging to never be saved.
Atop your mountainous ego,
I can't breathe -
So I let go.

RESONATE

Everything seems different for it took your departure to fix the curse.
Of course, somewhere you're still breathing but it's not shared through my lips.
Everyday I feel like your energy is being replaced.
Gone are the late night talks that were meant to find a forever we no longer seek.
Here now is the peace kept within me, as you're no longer within reach.
Who's to say you're at one with yourself but I'm now at peace.
You always felt faster than life and I felt tired of chasing something we labeled as ours.
The sweetness of being myself has finally replaced your sour,
Alone now are my quietest hours -
My tears no longer fall to give you power.

~~Ya got played~~
I'm only mine to save.

I'm in a lovely place right now, who you are to me is someone I can see myself with.
We've exchanged many powerful thoughts with each other and we will move mountains together. I'm not easy to manage, yet you let me express myself in the fullest of ways. I could be more brief with how I carry myself. Less into scripts but you don't wish that for me. I feel eternally blessed.

You've allowed me to see myself live in new ways. Through letting me be myself. I am so happy with you in my life. Your impact makes me want to do things that the world may call against my name, they may root against me, yet they don't matter. What truly matters to me is my commitment to your happiness.

I know faithfully that you've been there for me. You've been a home for my heart and my mind. I have a long life ahead of me and you've already heard some of the visions of my heart. I'll never feel alone for I want the best for us both. I know, through the care of our parents each side wants the best for their kid. I truly believe, that you're the best match to me. You see the same dreams. You have the same dreams as I do for our families. You have the same dreams as I do, for our legacy's.

Where I know, the tests will be there. They will come in small and big forms. There will be chaos, and we will get past the eye of every hurricane. We will never go without sharing how we feel for each other for the earth to quake. Together, if one goes a mile the other will go two and so on. Presently, I've never been happier in my life. I have endless appreciation for you and how you treat me. Your belief in me, the pride you have in calling me yours. I will remain loyal, to you and all those that make you happy. For I wish for that. That is how I will seek my happiness, because I know that as long as I have your support, my own family will see that I have become a stronger man. One who can see
past the fear, and do the most difficult tasks first. To speak his conscious dreams into life.

A striving image of a peacekeeper an honorable man. One that won't leave her side or her partners.

By not leaving yours, I won't leave your family either. I am thankful, you ask me questions whenever you wish to. The way you share openly what is on your mind. With all faith in God, I will achieve my lifelong dream. To be the best match another soul he's created. To serve her, and serve her family the same. I have you, so I have my purpose. It will require a lot of work, and you're worth every second of it all. Every second and every test.

RESONATE

You treated me like daily mail piling up till the postman wonders if you're still home.
I'm mixed with invitations you care nothing for, countless things you take care of online.
Applications you never cared for and reminders of seasonal garb asking you to subscribe to the Time's.
Forgetting the time you're living in.
Why won't you open me up after letting me know where to find you.
Were you left with many admirers who chose to defy you after confiding with you.
I'm not only parchment, I am a message.
Look at them soon, the post mark only tells you how I felt then.

Roundabout here and there, how bothersome can I be to you.
A share is what you seek?
A truthful story and statement to record for your records.
Sealed and shut.
Just like my lips.
Ask. Please do.
Keep asking. Begging of you so...
Mentally you won't unlock me.
Are you not the one,
Where is the one.
Who will understand where it all goes.
To sit and sit, listen then leave.
You don't understand, why am I paying you to hear me.
- therapy

RESONATE

I've loaded a pistol before, shot at targets.
Felt the cold weight of bullets, watched as they pierce through paper
so I won't have to imagine what they'd do to a door.
Thanks television.
Law & Order.
Who is on the other side.
A wall to collect the shells.
I'm walking on marble floors.
Heists on my mind.
Sweet mouth my way into vaults, you've been slipped of your keys.
That's not my fault.
Only my doing.
Highway robberies are too expensive.
Don't let me through, I'll take your time.
Leave you mystified.
In a flash of a second, you've given me the next set of moves.
Your cameras witnessed my spells, the many souls I've consumed.
In and out.
Contract complete.
Wondering how this revolver still has every bullet left, what a treat.

Wherever your mind is resting, your aura is missed.
You're in places we can't reach, yet we can feel as we reminisce.
Truthfully, there are many ways you are strong.
For this journey that you're on -
Everything seems to be what it should be and you become your own song.
Your will makes each lyric belong.
Every breathe you take, is a part of the chorus of your soul,
This Earth has its gifts, you faithfully cherish each part whole.
As you're connected to this world and your heart.
You will overcome in this time and the afterlife,
The many tragedies others fell from.
Your spirit will rise and so will those in with your company,
At each place your mind projects peace - we seek your energy and gracious harmony.
For you, there will always be love and never neglect.
Forever in our eyes, it is your courage we aim to protect.

Letting go of wanting, brings you closer to belonging.

With what you have and who you are.

AARAV CHOPRA

Wake up
Wake upp
Wake uppp
Wake upppp

RESONATE

The world wants it to reveal yourself,
As if being present is not enough.
Maybe they should have skipped teaching me history,
Or maybe they should take the technology I love away from me.
For I wish to be in secrecy,
Sending good vibrations near your doorstep,
If you're a loved in I wish to say these words in privacy.
As we call out to our smart devices,
Our choices.
Hey Siri. Hey Alexa.
Can you smile back?
They haven't developed you this way can you imagine that.
Maybe I should've been born before all this,
Further away even further back than when they played rock and roll and listened to Kiss.
Or Beethoven and Mozart without no words -
Imagine it.
We're further than we ever thought, building more and more these investors plot.
I'm okay with my love for antiquities.
Vinyl players tuned by amplifiers 33RPM's,
Tuning in viscerally.
Yet I can't deny the life I live for it's a blessing to just be.
A new decade 2020 -
I join my hands every morning and still only wish to pray peacefully.
The truest blessing is the air I breathe.
It's a privilege to be where I am, it's unfortunate that these words can't speak for all those
who inhabit Earth that you see.
On a screen, in your news, on your feed.
A modern reality.
Through my eyes this is what I type, and if you got this far -
This is what you now keep.
-
It's the antiquities I wish to own,
Vinyl players and coffee tables made by the men and women

with the wood that nature let grow.
I find that living.
For I still wish to come home to warm meals and no ads on the television.
Like I did when I was a child for I never knew the world was always selling me someone else's pipe dream.
A branded reality. I fall deeper and deeper into my shell.
I have never viewed the life the same through the virtual reality spell.

You can't crown every king - You shouldn't fill every throne. You can't praise every queen,
They've been known to act alone.

There will always be blood before every war,
The peace is breaking like every shooting star.
We have stopped identifying ourselves as who we are.
I'm no rebel.
I'm no hero.
I am not a saint.
Maybe the war starts here -
So is that really blood or is that paint?
Look beyond power and remove any freedom not in you, If it needs power, seek your own.

Have we the public forgotten of the routes we once took through the words and tales of another?
At times of loss and grief, vigils and folded prayer books - innocent people lost we still mourn. Some at the force of another's knees.
Some on trees, I kid you not, since Emmett Till I've been in disbelief.
Recorded in 55' said the textbooks in school -
How people of color were treated different than one another. As a kid I knew, "that's not cool."
I'd pray then and still do now - Please let this not happen any further.
To do this day I can hear as the train cars would echo

"approaching Fruitvale Station"
Like George we rallied for Oscar.
Generations spread by what's now been more than 10 years apart.
What time better than now to continue this fight.
Never look to anyone for ruining a life you are still in control of.

I have experienced the languages and cultures of so many.
I'm the pride and joy, of a beautiful immigrant family.
Yet my Indian tongue can mimic them all you see.
I am not a number. A lucky one.
I am one of many, only a part of it all - is that diversity?
We're not separated. To me? no one is to me.
I can talk. Let us all be free.
Even this daily bread, feels too much of a privilege to eat.
We all work to survive, we all work to feed.

I don't wish for you to forget these feelings and act as snow birds do. Please sit with us and resonate pass on this message -
That is all that we ask of you.
Remember we're together, in numbers -
We hear and recognize one other. The past has fought back countless times, so we must
continue to reclaim recover for every sister and every brother.
We have strength in numbers and have much to recreate.
Become an ally, peace love and positivity.
Ain't that great?

I have dreams of resting, on your collarbone,
Just to feel closer to your home.
Mind and heart.
As your breathes offer lullabies I drift away from melancholy.
I have run from so many people, I still run to this day.
I pace myself even in my dreams.
I'm beginning to fall in love with you -
So it seems.
For I wish to stay here, I wish to stay.
Help me understand my flaws,
Please remember me on your broken days.
I'll stand guard by your thoughts,
If I'm in love now, I was once broken -
No keys, just many locks.
I've laid myself down in places where I didn't belong.
Alone and cold singing songs of the strong.
Hold me now, hold me close.
I hear your heartbeat, I hear its rhythmic pulse.
Is this an oasis of thirst, have I been cursed.
I don't believe in loving lightly...
So why do I so in my dreams -
Lately it's only myself I've been fighting.
Or so it seems.

RESONATE

I remember the day as if it were yesterday, I won't tell anyone the date.
I will talk about our fate.
I was destined to love you and I simply had to play the patience game with the Lord, for He sent you first.
He waited for me to settle in afterwards.
Through the peace in your soul and the wisdom you've kept,
Your heart is one I respect and hope to protect.
I remember the day as if it were yesterday, I won't tell anyone the date. For the ones who have left and those I removed.
I chose you to love -
you and you and only you.

SOUL FOOD

We weren't made in a kiln,
A soul won't be found within.
What do you ask of this world, are you simply hanging on limb for limb?
Are you doing an honest mans work, freeing yourself of greed and sin?
Honoring the history of tradition, leaving what you can for your next of kin.
Or were you offered a different passage -
One with a silver spoon?
Will you take after these blessings to make more or will you forget too soon.
Of how you were raised and what you were given,
If the gift of life is not plentiful enough -
I can't see eye to eye with your decision.
-
Don't feel heavy when your caretakers have risen,
Folding your hands in prayer wondering if your selfish times will be forgiven.
Honor what's priceless for paradise offers no toll,
Invest in what you can't purchase and be grateful for your soul.

RESONATE

DISCLAIMER STRONG LANGUAGE & THEME USED

Let's talk about feminism.
Woah...don't go there, you're outnumbered in your gender pool.

Yeah? So what... There have been many occurrences where women have been directly put down in front of me. My profession leads to a lot of this. Sales is thought out to be a predominantly male field. I've run into many situations where I've kept quiet as I hear terms like, "slut," "whore," "cunt, "hoe," "homemaker,"...I can go on but I refuse to simply continue to type these degrading words as it harms my conscious.

It's terrifying how easy the "locker room," mindset really changed men. I'm not for that. I rather respect the reason I'm here. To bring light to what most men don't consider a serious topic. They say it's a "touchy subject," well...lol you still want to touch these women you objectify. Placing faith in your eyes for lust rather than respecting them as individuals with their own mind and body to own.

More men need to stand up for what's right and women's rights do matter. Hell...without them men wouldn't be here. The hashtag, "metoo" sparked this. I'm all for women standing up for themselves. The amount of powerful men dropping out of nowhere comes as no surprise. The amount of men not standing up for strong women who share their, "metoo" experiences scares me about the future of our nation.
Are men going to remain hush hush about this or will they take action and stand next to these strong women?

Strength here isn't applied to weights in the gym. How about the weight of your words on another's conscious? Regardless of sexual orientation. Praise both ends. Name calling, cat calling, all that jazz...needs to be tuned. By tuned I mean out. Reboot and respect.
Whatever happened to the honor shown to your mother and not a woman you see down the street?
Love every individual you encounter in life. Equally we're important to keep our surroundings safe. We can all make the world better. It's terrible knowing women are not
seen for their full beings. I stand with them. Not apart.

SOIL

Mystical eyes, a taming smile, behind her eyes lays a mind so uniquely wild.
I will leave her free in wanderlust, for pure is how she was styled.
The way she speaks of holding her own, her scent is one to be felt - those who know, will
speak of its healing, how it's a sensual cure.
Her hearts desires, the roots of her beliefs,
Methodical simplicity.
In a world of many, she has more to see -
I tell her challenges to stay ready.
Her battle cries are silent -
Her movements are calculated, she'll find all the peace.
Speak of no disbelief, for I once felt only the cold -
The warmth was never found in me.
The love I locked away, she has found and seeks to keep.
I've held her palms, her hands, her shoulders,
Yet I'll never hold her spirit as it smolders, she's an incense I wrap myself around.
When it's all over, leave her in ground.
Her wishes, her wishes are to be soiled, let the Earth know of her power,
Let's it core be where she's found.
For if you ask where she is with me,
Ask my heart who was it that made it skip a sound.

Water to wine mellow - I find you irreplaceable.
Time and time again proving timeless.
Take the wheel lead me in the same gear from here on.
Let me go no other pace, I'll side by your thoughts -
Stay loyal to this faith.
A gift has come to me that someone's here to stay.
I've been yearning for a safe zone to share energy with at times,
to each second coincidentally day by day. Time heals wounds but sometimes only a few words are needed to help.
I don't need four leaf clovers or trophies on my shelf.
I would love the continuance of your time, offer me that.
Even a second of you is enough for my health.

RESONATE

Scripting faces, Underlining <u>names.</u>
Striking through ceilings, Helping emulate the pain.
Make believe or not, most of it feels the same.
Interacting with one like this is more mind freeing than a block.
Thankful for the ideas leftover for harvest each time we talk.
Here's to the moment - "And that which sings and contemplates
in you is still dwelling within the bounds
of that first moment which scattered the stars into space."

When you're homesick, you think about the sky that made you.
When you're homesick, you feel like you've torn in two.
Then when you lay in bed, you light the ceiling on fire.
Just so you can witness, all of your demons watching you fight what's in your head.
It should never be as sad as this, no no.
You shouldn't have to go on, like this - no no.
So when you're homesick, you ask yourself of streets you miss.
Because this state, and your state of mind.
Are so different than the past times.
Hold on be grateful, be patient -
Don't be so wasteful. Of every breathe you take.
Just because you're homesick, it doesn't mean it doesn't mean no, no ...
That this place, is your resting state.

They were drowning,
Unlike us.
We were floating.
Their lungs were filled with lies so heavy of a love dark and crude, We never had the slightest chance of breaking trust.
Just favoring each others tells as signs of lust.
We were bound to set ourselves apart and we've mastered what they are still fearing.
Love.
The honest kind.
We hid from their evil eye, secrets of love kept in our mind.

(I FORGOT

        WHERE THIS

                WAS GOING)

RESONATE

My scars came from battles from those I love,
I requested their love and received only pain.
My ways were not aligned with their higher council,
Leaving fury as the only option left in my veins.
I've never been the one to preach my ways with those who showed no sense of belonging in my thoughts.
Rebellion is something that boils, so as you come to heal me remember what happens when you touch me like a pot.
Recall my ways of thinking, I've been abused by others and let them walk peacefully.
I've been mishandled by lovers and see that they still think of me.
For as long as I dream of harmony,
Those who question my freedom I will not let go of silently.
You will hear me beat my chest, rub the scars on my face.
Till these enemies are no longer within trace.

God granted me vision and I am blessed to see this life. Without your eyes, I can't see past mine. My eyes have minimal play, yours are as bright as my home in California where the sunshine prays. I wish to take you to my safe places, speak to you in the places that echo. Just places where I can tell you I love you and you would hear it surround you. I'd freeze in the glare of your eyes. I may have been spell bound since I saw them. God granted me vision to see beauty. He granted me this gift, to admire the vision of love kept in the hue of your eyes. How the waves move and your eyes don't. How the earth shifts its scale on a day and your love never fades. Cheers to your eyes, the reason I feel blessed to see and where I choose to remind myself of all the love I have for you in me.

RESONATE

See with your eyes the blessings,
The micro blessings too.
See with your eyes the peace -
That others have stolen from you.
You may not love yourself now.
You may not believe in tomorrow.
I believe in you, I believe in this day.
Serenity is not a long prayer,
It's only one word to say.
I hope you find peace, in yourself and this world.
I remember you happy and joyful.
May you always find the hope you long for.

Drifting in and out of consciousness,
I went from myself to a ghost.
Flat on my face, must've been because of the fake courage.
Too many smokes.
Drinks…mixing
Losing it all at the sink.
I've drifted with the ghosts.
They've claimed to be there, they were always in a world of their own.
So as I drift far from their reach now -
I hope they can find themselves home.
I've lost all hope -
Woke up cold.
This is the story of the blessing after -
Here is where it's told.
I'll be there, just not with the rest of the pack.

The world told me to rise, so I did. Not a suit and tie guy, not a forget to lock my door before I leave home either. Time to go make sure the key stays in my hand. Working for the day, thinking about the world and its charm on me. It's some weekday morning, I haven't even boarded the bus yet and my first social responses come from Outlook. What a way to live? Before I have a chance to speak to them, they're requesting something from me. I'm a pro fast walker and I've mastered my shrug.
I find the first seat, I've already said good morning to the driver. He nods, "Whatcha listening to this morning?" I smile and say, "Wasted Times," by The Weeknd. "It's Wednesday!" He exclaims.
I chuckled and moved on towards the first double open seat. Set my bag on one side and I on the other, lucky me.

Today seems like it will be just fine, maybe great, or none of the above and all just a transient waste. I make it safely to the office, I run a meeting everyday. I smile and laugh with the squad, they're my team. We discuss the results and all the other sales things. My life's a rerun until I pick up the phone. Everyday someone new, everyday someone that tries to throw me off or throwing me right into their fire. I felt extinguished leaving the shower this morning, remaining cool, collected, with clean delivery I recourse their issues.

This happens hour after after. Internal monologues of expletives help me escape the need for any medications. I reach in my pocket, yes I feel the key. I recall everything that's expected of me and the burdens of others sitting on my nerves.
The clock has flown it's 5:28, time to go home but I'm on a final call and hear, "Where are you from?" the woman asks. "I'm from California." I say with pride. "Where are you really from?!" "India." Again with pride.

"I would've never guessed it, wow, you have no accent. I would've guessed you're Caucasian!" My face turned into the text emoji with dashes for eyes and an underscore matching mouth. Ya know? -_-

So I packed up my belongings, thanked Ms. Never Call Again for her time and get ready for my next round of extinguishing. Can't wait to go home and kiss my pup.
Nothing will make me feel better than that and the hoodie sweats combo after a shower. What a day, just another day. Just to hold this key.

RESONATE

I rush for your taste,
Like 5 o'clock whiskey.
Everyone screams happy hour and I just want to make it home before rush hour.
Never chasing my liquor, only chasing your love.

My scars came from battles from those I love,
I requested their love and received only pain.
My ways were not aligned with their higher council,
Leaving fury as the only option left in my veins.
I've never been the one to preach my ways with those who
showed no sense of belonging in my thoughts.
Rebellion is something that boils, so as you come to heal me
remember what happens when you
touch me like a pot.
Recall my ways of thinking, I've been abused by others and let
them walk peacefully.
I've been mishandled by lovers and see that they still think of me.
For as long as I dream of harmony,
Those who question my freedom I will not let go of silently.
You will hear me beat my chest, rub the scars on my face.
Till these enemies are no longer within trace.

You speak of worry as if it lives on your skin, let it not fold as you live.
Speak of worry in your mind and not out through your being.
Don't let it spite enter where light belongs, we glow in the radiance of a new day and do wrap under the watch of moonlight come night fall.
Worry must not take over your being, let stress find its way to reinforce your ability to overcome.
For a task may offer you a blessing a worried mind will not find.
Be strong and courageous in the face of adversity, be mindful of its ability to change you.
Let no man tell you they are better, let no man tell you they're perfect.
For they are worried about your ability -
And how you hold the potential to surpass their expectations.
All while rewarding yourself, and letting worry sit in your mind to drive your heart.
Thinkers and doers find a way to put things together as others let themselves fall apart.
Everyday is formative, everyday you can win.
Let worry sit in your mind, don't let it be the reason to feel uncomfortable in your own skin.

DELIVERY TO DELIVER & PORTION TO POTION

I haven't lost touch with my senses,
You could draw my blood and I'll prove to you I'm myself.
Not yours, not yours.
You scarred me as you pleased -
There have been marks left by me,
Right where you wish to see, in places I no longer have reach.
In my dreams -
I've danced away from the bullets in Havana.
Searching to destroy what you're not able to see.
Try to detonate me, slowly, I'm figuring out your patterns.
I'm just a reminder of reincarnation in living form.
How I've been blown to bits and still belong.
A painful diary.
I am not the only one to see, a tragedy.
Where you once again come to draw blood from me.
Deliver me to the chosen few, the healers of the make believers.
Hypnotized or chastised.
Mix to make the potion,
Every night your ghost drifts into my sleep.
Paralyzed.

ALL HEARTS DON'T PLAY FAIR

My heart is an empty minefield,
Communicating with sirens of compassion.
Yielding to lovers in my lifetime has never come easy -
Approachable I've been, some I've met and let in.
Oftentimes belonging remains questionable.
For our past belongs with us, our beds sinless.
Only a fool walks into a problem asking for time to be taken back.
Decisions, decisions.
Walk into my heart, take what you must -
Please never do so anonymously,
I must know who to trust.
Through their smile, I've learned the language of fire in their eyes
as they displace lust.
Truth be told, all I know is their souls don't belong with mine.
I'll harness my love, hold locks of chastity.
My heart is an empty minefield,
I don't play fair either.
Watch out for the tripwire.

I will always have a soft spot,
In a heart I keep open for souls.
There's no closed sign in these quarters,
I don't love in halves. Just making sure others feel whole.
I cry when fathers see their sons,
In his countries colors after months.
Like mothers who tear as they see their child,
After a healthy birth they see their blessings -
Finally in their arms forever, a sign of love they can touch.
I will always find love, in many souls not just one.
For if there was a love to have, I wish for all of us to love each other,
As if inside we're all made from the same blessings -
As the other soul next to us.

PARANOIA, PARANOIA

Right now I want you, to be swept off your feet and brought to me.
For this distance from a star like you has not been kind to me.
A nebulous energy now surrounds me.
The ghouls of my past are present as time is passing - I'm not a fan of this wake.
Or of their presence as they test what's to come of my fate.
I've heard from elders, journeys like our lives brings some into a gruesome state -
Where happiness may not belong on every given day.
Yet every calendar will continue to be printed.
Date after date after date.
It will all weigh on our skin, I'll attest to that fact.
I've never struck another with my fists, I do so well disappearing leaving no tracks.
The beauty in my power is not masked as a man who lost some of his mind, I've been foiled by those I cannot see.
I'll find myself thinking and balancing, one or the other.
For steady is all I wish to be.
Why must they capture me, leaving me in debt with the business of futurity.
Freezing me hopelessly, tormenting the possibilities of my lonely star who can offer solace to me.
Am I just another soul, welcomed by this energy?
I refuse to become a statistic, yet here I am calling out for my freedom endlessly.

Empty streets teach me more than the busy ones,
I know this to be true.
Seattle isn't as warm as California is,
Tell them some better news.
How does it feel to be on an island no matter what address you're attached to.
Whether solo or speaking of a family tie what is left for you?
I flatten my hands and show you no fist,
God if you're hearing this, am I headed towards you or another's list.

SAPIOSEXUAL

Through empty nights and no love,
I've forgotten how companionship tastes on my lips.
For the next person I touch, will love me like a virgin.
For I've been afraid for so long, as I've heard the journeys others go through.
I've seen people quietly mold themselves into likable beings,
Have they held onto the meaning of my name before they wish to make me sing?
I'm so removed from the choruses of heartstrings, no living being can send life back into me in one night.
I don't need a bed to make peace, my mind has become my home.
If you're here to love me, tell my nerves you're here to stay.
If you're here to save me, tell my heart your name honestly first.
I cannot let you near me, if I can't savor you from afar.
I may want what's rare, I find so much more behind ones eyes -
One day I'll remember belonging, and it won't always be like this.
The patience I have now, will speak volumes to the next person I choose to lay with.

Careful caution lies ahead.
I wish that's what the world would have spelled out to me before you tried to fix me with some *head*.
I've been triggered for years, years of saving this for later.
Yet I won't let you live in my mind, my mind no longer serves as a cemetery.
A grave digging soul, entered into my rented home.
A difficult stay.
I was on my last bit of hope, you didn't need to yell.
I held this all in my heart, and never let my mind spell its tale.
Hellish. All of it.
I avoid it all now like a plague, mattresses no longer feel comfortable with another next to me.
Or on top of me.
I'm a **human**, not a *freeway*.
Paved the way for my living, never hitchhiked for love.
Don't *ride* me, don't think you can fix me.
In homes not blessed, the devil finds a way in.
Your eyes held a demon, in my heart is where you let it stay.
Victimized.
My soul hasn't harmonized with another since.
For my body was rubbed like clay, then broken and shattered to pieces.
I was motionless as my mind was sent into places I was *speechless*.
Not a word. No pleasure.
Why give me this fate, why come to "heal" when you came to steal.
An argument never made up, pain and mental scars left to feel.
Who will want to touch a skin that no longer feels like his own.
I've been searching for a seamstress.
Left to sow my heart alone, it's near complete, nearly taken a decade to find confidence.
Some belief.
Goodbye demon, I hope you can see my smiling as you're finally disappearing.

Who is in the mirror of a home that's rented,
A body that's standing but in this home he will not be cemented.
This hardwood cost some blood and sweat equity.
Stainless steel, oh that came with the place, and it's as cold as I feel.
Somewhere on this Earth, as it spins I'll find my mirror.
For I have grown tired of the man who knocks, on the last day of the month, an hour early when we turn back the clock.
He's come to collect, what I've already set aside.
He's rented our pockets, don't we pay for every door he knocks.
We know what he wants, no surprise.
-
Knock Knock

AARAV CHOPRA

Shadows crease over my my pitted face,
Doing all that I can some marks still remind me of the taste.
Of every fall that I was too impaired to save.
Where I begin to smile, my frown will be watching from close by.
Karma tends to remind of old reckless habits -
Calling out the passerby's.
I have made friends with distance,
How I enjoy turtleneck sweaters for they cover my throat.
T-shirts for the four walls of home,
Only there does my face glow.
I'm no longer one to shake every single hand.
I've heard from a few in the crowd, they've made their judgments before they met the man.
I will bring questions, as they relay doubt.
If you're only here to save yourself, my anxiety will show you out.

RESONATE

We may only seek a healers direction in life, for its only work we know how to do.
We may lead and build things beyond our wildest dreams, but where are we to rest our heads
away from the unseen.
A soul we can just be with, in peaceful enchanting solitude.
Where we feel present and cured -
Welcomed, never lured.
Tasteful to our five senses,
As sweet as the only item at Café du Monde,
Soothing to hear like MJ, even when brought back today.
As beautiful as your lovers eyes setting on yours.
As soft as their lips offering words.
A scent you'd wish to take with you when you're gone.
A kind of healer that could remove old tears from a pillowcase.
Place them near you, don't let their efforts go to waste.

Thankfully I'm here, the days turn on their own.
I've yet to be taken from this zone.
The mental state of being offered a lie,
A reason to turn my world around while presently dealing with strife.
My own reasons of balancing wrongs versus rights.
Sleep is not only for the rich, what about the wise.
Today I walk with bags under my eyes.
Coffee beans brewed to make it alright.
A new day, is no reason to fight,
My eyes made it through just another night.

It's crazy when you lose ones trust,
Have they let you fall -
At a leafs pace to the ground bargaining with infinity as you land.
So far I'm still floating,
Can we wish for the same things,
I don't need you to involve the almighty,
Let's just sing.
Spare that even -
I need your memories, old and new in my head no more thought of a ring.
Is this trust bound by a possession, or will you lift me back up to your truth.
I wasn't there to harm, were you just there to assume?
-
Recluse

ACQUAINTED

The sound of her voice, a soft serenity offering cadence's full of melodies.
As her eyes bloom in front of me, my soul was sent drifting into places I've never seen.
I was falling in spring, over a burning sky in May.
My heartbeat skipped for the first time on that unforgettable day.
As her grace layers in my mind, I smile and think of how beautiful she remains.
Etching deeper into my conscious thoughts, enamoring the blood in my veins.
Where she sits I wish to lay, where she sleeps I wish to stay.
I've let years go by, just to feel this way.
Undoubtedly I pray, that when she needs love -
I will continue to send mine her way.
For I have no more requests for heavenly gifts around me,
Aside from those we both care for to live in flourishing health and harmony.
This joy, this serenity, offered by the one and only…___?

RESONATE

You gotta know where your feelings are, gotta know where you're going.
If you're falling for someone who are they after it not you.
Don't fold your heart for someone that doesn't think like you.
Convince until it hurts and then move on is what you ought to do.
We've lived a long life, loved many people and things.
Don't let your inner voice go, it really wants to sing.
Don't be stripped, don't be damaged.
It's all a lot to take in - keep some love for you within.

I'll catch the sunrises for you, finish your dreams,
If they are to be nightmares -
I'll bring you back some light.
Allow me to open your darkness after I've said hello to our sky.
Folding away the pain you've felt overnight.
Softly brushing your skin as if we're cleansing away yesterday's fight.
For you've done so much,
You're apart of this world -
As of late only a lampshade and I are aware of your touch.
Through every season, through every dream, through every nightmare -
I'll catch these sunrises for you, everyday until you're there.

You drew the plays and I followed through.
All your shots I scored for you.
Typical overhead mentality you played me.
Forgot my sweat equity and casualties.
The glare in your eye every time I put my head down as I passed.
Disingenuous vibes, none of this would ever last.
You're left with all the trophies,
And I could do no good with what you left me.
- Benched

To harness future success one must expect to be trespassed by loss. You may feel blessed, beaten,
set aside from the steady path. Never deny the shapes of your shadows.

Let them glare those with evil eyes and take your light to a merry path.

Remember advancing to success means burning off the many bridges that proved to never last.

No person deserves to wrap you around their finger. Your heart will never wrap around the wrong home for too long. It too will have a voice of its own.
unloving is as painful as accepting a new love

I offered you a key as a sign of trust,
You'd turn the door only to ask for lust.
I really hope you marry the next person you do this to.

One of the most beautiful moments to me is when someone tells me they were saved by love.
Think of anything you could be saved by in harm's way but if love is the answer then the source isn't physical. It was passed onto you.

You could have a six figure debt then get bailed out in cold hard cash but take a long term relationship and money won't change a damn thing.

If money can fix your heartbreak we have different priorities.

The ones worth loving make it difficult once it becomes far too easy to love them.
Not for their selfish reasons,
But to see if you're willing to continue to battle for them.
May your loyalty evolve, and your love never end.

Love
Needs
New
Thrills

Love
Needs
More
Practice

Love
Should
Never
Be
Routine

Nowhere,

                                        Somewhere

Speaking without no logic,
Having nothing to say yet bragging about it.
People just talking about their likes and comments.
Ruining their dopamine levels, their parents think their fans are just humans that have no life.
Constantly yelling at them to get on with their time.
Liar liar the bank said you just failed another wire.
Why is your need to be famous so dire?
Selling your life to the highest buyer.
-
Notoriety feat. S. Talati

RESONATE

While we're holding each other,
Our love is directed at another.
Each one loves me a little bit more every day,
Why can't I put them down and hold just you?

____ liked your post.
____ shared your story.
____ RT you.
____ pinged you into this room.

Never let your lover feel less special than the digital you.
How will you focus on their soul, how will they hear you for you.
Can you put down your devices, and just be you.
Tell them something the servers won't store,
Tell them pieces of your life that others won't come to explore.
You're to be loved, not to be liked.
You're to be heard, not to be misquoted.
You're to be seen, not to be screenshotted.
You're a human being, not an internet spokesperson.
Day and night.

There are not enough good men crediting the great men.
There are not enough great men respecting the good men.
All men are none the wiser.
We wage wars on each other, inflict harm to those we aren't alike.
So it goes, women be able to tell us apart.
Another's guilt has become yours and somewhere in between
you've lost before you could start.
Avoid being labeled as ~~temporary~~.

Lights!

Rolling….

Action….

The devil's in his past turned him loose onto this Earth five years ago, and he begrudgingly found himself failing day by day. Until she came, and said he was to change for himself or else she'd never be found again. There is a stream of consciousness akin to that of a river bending in his mind. There's a forest wrapped in the mountainsides in front of him, the fog to the left and the rise of the sun inbound.

It's dawn. His red eyes have lusted for the sunrise. His feet wore blisters from his journey, the elevation he found himself on was only meant for waterfalls. He wished to be above water, he heard the story of Noah's ark and here he is atop a mountain. He's heard myths of people walking on water but what about being above it all and looking to the depths of the fall. He wished to be where no man had ever gone.

The journey began 991.8 miles away. He began this journey in California, the final destination he prayed he'd make it. He never knew what he'd see but he knew the reason why he was fighting. As a child, he may have felt lost in the noise, the only peace he found himself in was within the trees. How they protected him from feeling like he was closer to anything than the soil he stood on. There was a spirit in him, something kindred.
Bewildered by the beauty of woman, he knew something about her that no one knew.
The climb felt difficult at times, he felt like he was blinded by her light but he never gave up. He drank from the streams and left out the grains for the animals in the forest.

He was only doing what he new would ritualize her rise. He gave away to the forest things they had never seen. A man so restless in determination and giving. The animals saw him, they guided him, he felt their eyes drawn into the madness in his. They knew he wanted to be there, bridal veil trails. Sitting above the forest, watching it all flow below.
He knew that her spirit was twined in the air that was fresh and she would be there at the top. She was found, at the end of his journey and his heart felt at ease. She offered him her arms and

he felt like his heart was finally quenched of it's thirst. He was capable of spending years in nothingness, so he drew from the faith that he found and rushed to her.

He knew that this sunrise was worth the purity in her heart and her kiss gave him the cure he needed. The blisters faded, his body was renewed. His heart found the meaning of hers, and he laid down hearing her streams and felt her skin soft as the petals he collected on the way. The best gift on Earth, was the soul sent to her body for him.

Sewn together after some bad wishes,
Their skin is no longer soft, quilted almost.
A patchwork job at best.
Naysayers smile at you and a glimpse of Heath Ledger's Joker
rampantly breaks your smile.
Harbingers of the past have warned us, that such beauty
wrapped in misfortune - will break the strongest of minds.
Who are theses wingless souls crooked for, why have they not
removed themselves from guilt and disharmony.
Have we quietly fostered ourselves into their indecencies amongst
all the other things that we let go.
Are they too close to the ones we send for heaven -
Will the angels we love cry when their hands no longer remain
clean.
For they've played and sinned with the now plagued demons.
As midnight creeps upon the hallowed grounds of my home.
Where I feel safe, a raven nests by my side.
A blend of angel and demon, an aura you'll never find.
Nevermore.

RESONATE

So it began when you were born,
Under the sunshine or the rain.
Sing your name in between these lines,
Help arrives from the sweet children chorusing along as they play.
May your life be a lullaby -
Interesting and luminous on the day's I feel gray.
Tell me there's no one like you,
How you will begin to agree -
All signs leading to you offer me peace and tranquility.
Kindly take these words,
Observe them when you please.
May this new year around the sun, be the most fortunate year for you to see.
A journey you'll write as you continue to succeed.
Remembering where you came from, as you head towards who you'll be.

Skeletons don't have to live in your closet when you carry a hatchet in your mind.
Drown out your failures and replace them with success stories.
You deserve to write open letters of forgiveness to yourself.

RESONATE

She takes away anything that isn't her,
Unknowingly.
It's as if the room is still in a red hue and we're staring at film develop.
Together awaiting the memories as they surface.
From the smiles to the tears I just know I'm not alone,
Going through every emotion known to man together.
Not alone.

Deny my meaning, but did you ask your heart before you made your choice?

RESONATE

When he's ready to love you forever,
He'll be on his knees before he asks you to be on yours.

Feel it between your veins, when they ask you to read between the lines.
I don't believe in the plans made best for one party on paper -
If I'm the one signing for it as they take my heart away.

RESONATE

I love your chase so much,
I never sought to love myself this much.
Truth be told it will never be enough.
I've been around and around in my head,
I won't let you bitter you shouldn't be left.
For dead inside or for worse.
In these streets or these sheets.
Said it before, I'll work to edify and dote.
There are notes / inside my mind you know -
I'm giving them away / How can I define what hasn't been loved all the way.

I feel too much, I trust your soul so much.
I am a soldier waiting to be fallen by your touch.
Feed me now, I am an empty lover.
Find me now, I should be under your covers.
Hold me now, I am not for staying still.
Alone.
Come to me, I don't want to escape my minds memories and thrills.
You're a dream I can't have and I must admit.
You'd be better off with him, and for me I'm left to imagine what if.
What if…

Only place I find peace is split.
Splitting your legs / leaving my hand on your back arches.
Leave a scar to feel, claw a journey on me.
I could love you from here no matter what the cost is.

Who put a price on your freedom I'll take you to where you're priceless.
Send vibrations through your thighs, tender kisses on your naval.
In the heat of it all whispering all the sweet nothings / oh, you've been so exhausted.
No matter what the cost is.

I could love you from here.
I'll pull a chair to watch you know where it all is.
I know where it all started.
Highway robbery of a heart, you sped away and I've been chasing you for the longest.
My mind continues to spin / All I want to do is sin.
I don't want us to make promises.
Sing for me,
So I could play you back 1,000 miles away.
No matter what the cost is / send my life back to me I'm heartless.

RESONATE

My verbal stabs leave no impression on a mind made of steel.
I doubt you're ready to listen for it's never what you want or care to feel.

I was raised strong, I was raised to be brave.
To not question but survey. To harness the pain, to never get played.
To be rigid, to fort my worth.
To respect and protect, the name I hold.
To heal and serve, those who couldn't see a new to their views of old.
These gifts came from a woman, these gifts came from no man.
Shielded by the memories of the breadwinner and my belly saver.
The tiresome efforts of motherhood.
No one else would do for me what my mother would.
How to raise men to see through the names and genders and to love everyone the same.
Carefully yet wholeheartedly.
A marvel to me, another soul destined to walk right into heaven let no one deny.
The creator of my destiny, taught me to be strong.
Taught me to be brave.
I live to shine a light on our home, so that she can witness the fruits of her labor take us so far everyday.
No man taught me how to do, what one woman could.
To care, through any mistake. To pray, in goodness and despair.
Shuffling my feet no more, I reserve the pain.
Anything to let her see every daylights warmth - just so she can smile and remember the day.
Every memory that I forgot, she knows.
Everything we never had, will be what she'll hold.

RESONATE

Hollow tips through pierced skulls,
Have you jumped the gun?
I only met translucent loops around ear lobes and noses filled with fun.
Cultures to remember and respect.
Why do others see it as mystical.
Jewelry revealing medievals.
Times of the modern kind.
Hollow tips piercing skulls,
In war torn lands where no plaintiffs sing.
Defendants load shells, freedom was never meant to ring.
No assumptions in a trigger, all a choice.
No assumptions in a piercing, all a choice.
Let each body live their own story,
Let each bullet live it's tale.
Yet why do we care for ammunition, when the trigger man is slated for hell.
We judge a tattoo, we judge a piercing.
Yet loaded shells we pay no attention to, who are we licensing.

And I hope,
That today you would find me and out of this our love would be born.
Yet I know,
We are neither here nor we're there
but at the end of it all I suppose.
Who is to know?

Texts only do so much to share,
Swiping I don't even know who is there.
So I go,
Out into this world looking for dream girls knowing I will be in love.
Some day.

Here I know, who is to hold my hand a hand hasn't been held.
For I don't, appreciate the touch.
Of another so much, let it be for a fragment of time.
I don't remember, the many hugs I've given away.
Yet I store, anyone who walked hand in hand with me everyday.

It's their memories that eat me away.
I wouldn't know how else it could be said.
My soul wishes to find, one that will make it all new again.
New in the sense of the memories my friend.
A lover not a menace, yet I like the sassy ones most.
Guessing this is just an open letter to me saying my heart would love a new host.

We'll trade nights.
Where you won't sleep.
then I won't sleep the next.
We'll trade fights. Exchange the gloves.
You'll heal my heart, I will heal your aches.
We're only ours till the end. The end.
Again and again.
More than our vows, we've had to dig deeper for each other within.

My glorious love, my secret sin.
I'll be never the one to share the name of your bliss.
Will you hold, my hand till the end of time.
I don't ever want to be separated or say that I miss.
We'll trade nights.
Where we won't make love, we'll just hold each other and look at the eyes.
The eyes that make everything, alright.

Where you feel pensive,
I feel submissive.
To your desires, needs, cravings, do you find me admissible.
I'll meet you at the middle of your favorite song.
Bridging closer to the chorus of your heart.
I'll be smiling for you'll be healed.
Are you still pensive?
I've thought of how I would love you before.
Consent is what I've wished for.
A journey caravanning your smooth skin.
I've only felt chills like this where my mind was lifted.
There's lots to soil away, I've been told to just let it sit in -
The Earth.
So may I explore your worth.
I don't wish to say that I've travelled far and wide.
Just want to be here.
Twilight hours, you don't reach to turn on anything if not for me.
Am I admissible?
Let us be clear tonight.
I feel submissive.
I am asking to be taken over,
By you.

RESONATE

Empty seasons, trust I feel that they all are beautiful but empty.
The warmer it gets, the more pain I hear.
The colder it gets, the more I hear of the regret.
The more it falls, the more I hear that it's too beautiful. To die.

Another day, another sad song.
Let me sing and live.
Another day, another lie caught.
Humanity humanity...why must you try to do me in?
I'll catch you, I'll save you.
I'll blanket you, I'll feed you.
Angels will bless me, demons will entrap you.
You'll find me. In your emptiness.
As a savior.
Yet no one comes to me.
Mistakes I'm still paying for.
Don't go down that path, it's layered with fuses and contempt.
Few weeks later, I'll come to bandage your head.
"How are you so quick to heal?"
What you're going through, I've forgotten how to feel.
-
Numb

Depression is a heavy burden, I went years without learning its true meaning on my name. I've hidden from it, talking about happy is too good and easy for me. So that's where I go. Y'all want the smile and not the woes. Who really wants to hear the pain age in me as I grow. However, there are souls who've tried. To put balance into my name.
Outlier. Best they could come up with. I've lost. Myself. Before. I walked into their doors. I've cried and written long emails to explain it all before. Before before and before.

You're no longer welcome here anymore. I don't need your stories or therapy. I walk into souls that are pleasurable not payable heresy. How can you conquer a mind that is my own. I don't want your temporary beliefs. I've sat in your rooms.

The only thing that raised my eyebrows, was that you still couldn't figure me out. Took your prescriptions and poured them all out. Liquor too. What else do they wish for me to do?

I've listened and I've listened. Hollow points through my chest. Can't find my pain?
That's why I have told you for so long. You're never getting in my head. I don't want to trust you. You've labeled me, yet never allow me to ask. How are you?

Anger slips into my mind as I recall your name,
A friend not my foe.
Ironically I hate you now, yet I loved how you
sat in my dreams.
I'd lull myself to sleep - wondering how long this battle would last.
Awake you were never fun, I'd immediately find a smile to mimic
the one I lost.
Depression my old friend, I believe you live rent free.
For as long as I have lived, I hadn't known you.
I found you in an attic, buried away.
In a place I never crawled to.
Standing up is never how you wished for me to meet you.
Ironically. Everything we do is in disbelief.
The two sides of me you control.
Happiness doesn't require a cure, it's ailment is you.
You my old friend.
Time to pay, I've come to collect.
I hold the blade you won't know how to skip this debt.

RESONATE

A moment was taken, a mind was shocked.
I felt like I was to walk on egg shells, and I received the news which brought emotions of new mental blocks.
Where I felt low, my sisters offered their fire passing their torch so that I may no longer continue to sulk as I walk.
There's bliss on the other side, it's never too late to see the fate.
To hear a beating heart that shares your blood, and your name.
You may cry today, but the cries you wish to hear will come from another.
The fingerprints are still being passed, there are new souls being born.
As we pray and seek wholeness,
There will be a day, that a child is given to you so that you will feel reborn.

THE MIDNIGHT SPECIAL

12:12am the man sat knowing his train was to board a few hours ago, he tore apart the ticket. On his boots one of the knots had come undone and he realized there's yellow sticky trails leading him. "What happened to the days he asked?"

"Where folks would simply leave love notes on tables for others to read someday. The hell is this Juicy Fruit doing at the bottom of my boot. Goodness."

"Those times are still here!" Someone cries out in a deafening shout. Scribbling their name on a piece of parchment. It read, "Medora."

The man quickly exclaims back, "Why are you handing me this! I've a train to catch, and I'm frightened of you for how terribly loud you just yelled across the station."

"I offered you my name, something to take with you as you go Mr." His face turned red, he reminded her that he tore up his ticket.

RESONATE

January flowers, February lilies -
March has it's St. Patrick's clovers.
Make room for the lovers.
I remember the bodega, two streets left of 5th
He had Hershey's kisses and buttered toast ready to go.
It was not the 14th of the month most breakup -
Just a happy joyful day in the neighborhood.
New Yorkers talking loudly, kids riding bikes.
I wonder what the soil felt like last year, when no one was there to water you.
All year round, you were there.
Flowers in your mind, peace in your soul.
Come one come all, it's time to grow.

I've heard of stories in the past of her ways,
Through folks that chose to make a temporary stay.
Will you request some part of my past that you wish to keep for your now.
Do you simply need an eye for eye?
Do you seek a hope renewed. A heart returned to its glory.
I'm unsure of the lover or villain you seek.
Don't send your heart to me.
I've mended more than you, I need you to see this one through.

RESONATE

Turn the key, fester your emotions -
Understand the home in the mind.
Behind the blinds is the universe outside -
Behind your eyes is the place of high tides and low.
Waves clashing against thoughts, nerves seeking moments to reduce your cravings.
What are you craving?

I no longer feel the strokes, of ones brush against the easel of my skin.
The story does not portray me in color,
Or do they now hold me in quest.
Where are you from?
It's always been loaded and now it feels too much.
For if I say where I am from, will I be deemed that I'm worthless?
Why can't they say hello to the smile in front of them?
Where I am from is the last memory of happiness in my head.
That's where I am from.
-

Ask about my day, not my origin please

RESONATE

Rebuilding myself has been difficult,
I've found myself here again
The pieces are rougher around the edges,
My experience in putting myself back together has nearly spread three decades.

How many times will I have asked myself of my purpose in all of this?
Am I misinformed or informed. Did I source it or you?
Was it told in good faith, or was it all shared to me in angered haste.

United I may no longer stand. I haven't felt global.
Yet I feel at home, alone. Like you.
I revolt through more learning, education, subscription to truth. I open myself to those of
opinions, other than what I call my own.
Yet when it comes to my name or my passage,
Only my sins can I atone.
Only for my voice, may I vote.

I've passed the truths, the messages, the many countless stories.
I've verified, I've researched, I've felt sick to my stomach at times & maybe you have too.
I've sent in my census, once a decade they plan trillions to take care of you.

Every morning I pray, knowing sunrises like this exist.
Asking for something safer than what's here today.
A safer place to rebuild & stay.
A conversation where I'm valued, not treated like clay.

I'm tired of rebuilding and blending into the frame.
Don't cleanse my minds palette, there's more than just color to my name.
For it is enough, today, and every other day.

THE GREATS ARE FALLING

We're losing the ones who never had a way,
Yet did more than just pave a way.
They've been thrown against the concrete,
Jailed and asked to repent for being.
Asked to silence themselves when their insides would scream.
They've battled through scar forming paths and journeyed till their resting place.
Yet before their wake, they awoke millions.
Not all scars are visible.
Generations will pass the tale.
Not all will forget their mother's story,
Their fathers smile.
A grandfathers sweater to a grandmothers sweet palm on your skin.
We should not forget our heroes, the ones who carry their spirit in our veins.
Leave the world better than how you may feel within.
There's work to do, the greats are falling.
Their voice mustn't end, hear them as they're calling.
The echoes of their search for freedom, beats in you.

Our bite may not be as strong as another's.
We must not forget the power held in a pack.
The might left in our hearts when we choose to collide with
another's energy can eat
away to form insurmountable maladies.
If we remain stranded on this ever-changing Earth -
We will never proceed to understand it's change.
Surface levels are not friendly,
They are reminders of the balance we wish to free ourselves from.
For as the world breeds it's energies,
In dark and light forms we must believe -
That a lonely path, is full of unsurvivable insecurities.
There are ways to grow, no mind should be left in soil.
Without an ocean of love,
To help rise taller than the trees.

Every voice is welcome through these doors.
Skip the time zones and ask the time of your heart.
It will tell you it was here, on this Earth - your journey of being enough continued or it truly began to start.
Remember to skip on the pedestal chats today, thank you Mia for the awareness.
Bring yourself and your mates, thank you Harry for how you came to reminisce.
We have lyrical warriors, we have healers present.
Today is our gift, our tomorrow is being built.
I thankful for time zones, for I now have memories of tomorrow through my mates.
Don't ever give up, not in this reflective moment.
You are enough, a springing flower laying in nature's soil not cement.

RESONATE

I grew up around show stoppas,
And go gettas.
Big steppas big action types.
No wonder we're all rising now -
People are not mystified.
From The Bay to the Universe -
Gerald broke more than a couple barriers -
Air strike flows watch your territories we bringing harriers.

Maybe if you respected our soul you would be able to listen clear -
Commonalities present a mind heart and your ears.
Continue to celebrate the ones you know -
Separate your fears and be ready to grow.
We demand diversity now, we have it in The White House hope it journeys to the globe.
Be aware of your power -
Set yourself on a journey of hope.

Proper thinking and self love -
Remove yourself from debbie downer drugs,
Adopt a local rescued pug.
I lived with a few, Kasper and Popeye -
Where the Albay's said grace.
Just a story from a California kid that just went back to a clean face.

We all got caught up in affiliations,
Colors and parties forgetting our names man.
Picking up the words where another left off.
Who cut them off.
Maybe it's not for this everyday worker, to write his ass off.
But -
No one wants to talk to you unless you got your mask on.
Hol' up no Gambino we might be masked on till 3005.
Got all these questions and thoughts people shook and wonder why.
Should've seen the look in your eyes when I read you like a book.
Ma's recipe said few extra pinches of salt - she never needed a book.
Hand me your identity, social and cvv -
Prior hustles don't make me, me.
My heart is my sole affiliation been trying to welcome me.
Back.
Everyday.

Welcome to the land of misogyny -
Notoriety through ad space content distribution algorithmic rich.
What an analogy.
Drop this, cop that. Rep it once share it & tag -
Oh they won't repost you but they'll respect you when you pay their ask.
They got somewhere. They brought you along.
Heavy heavy hands every time that you shop.
Don't worry young soldier, you'll figure it out.
Just keep thinking about the final destination-
Escape appropriation.
Form your own alliances - get down with your soul and ask yourself who can you be for
this world.

Don't be read like a book, when your cover changes daily.
The locks in your mind don't need smiths they need you baby.
Let them witness you early and then line up when it's too late.
Fate would have it that they'll still show up to congratulate.

RESONATE

I think in months while you worry about the seconds to a traffic light.
Decades form legacies, don't send me your hatred tonight.
It'll bottle up and fester, constantly my mind is ready to fight.

Ego & fear stops us. Dealing with those two alone with yourself is a battle the final text is waiting for you to win. While writing we make the levels, the game's final boss is truly you.
Not the audience. There is no high score, the only trophy you can gain is the completion of the never ending tale of your soul.

Rejection is a neighbor I've befriended.
Yet never comes into my home.

MELANCHOLY

You were meant to be saved, last.
As if you were chosen, to be the strongest and there was no reason for a coin toss.
They pushed you, so far away from the edge.
There you went, trading your happiness for the next pledge.
For whatever wouldn't carry you into an end.
Falsifications of your own -
Damnation in your home.
Plenty of lies filled you whole.
Too many wrongdoers in your soul.

Give me a little time, just a little time -
For the smile to come back.
For your heart to smile again.
Your heart to see new blood.
Did you feel and forget.
New memories, new bodies in your head.
Graves in your fingers, how many ghosts have you shaken hands with.
How many.
Reapers vs. gatekeepers.
Locked fists, eyes black.
Your demons don't harm me, they have qualities I don't lack.
Your hearts stitched, I've brought you back.

Let's echo this fact - We all want each other to win.
May we all find our inner voice, I pray you all continue to sing.
Candles lit, vibes right.
Mother ocean, I'm here - send the tides so we can harness your depths tonight.

Resurrection is not necessarily an afterlife act, there are ways to seek revival while you're living. Focusing on past failures only proves that they can anchor you.

Stepping through the acceptance of your fortune, removing the anchor is the next step in your fated journey. A lover, a loss in the family, a skipped set of words from another party that leads to a break / pause. Whether you're seeking for the world to handle your woes for you or another soul, it doesn't get better until one wishes for it to themselves.

I read an Instagram share not too long ago, it read, "Manifest, but do the work too." Not here to end hopes and dreams, I've read and seen too many people celebrating the creation of their vision board yet the work isn't done. It's great, to look up the images of things you wish to see materialize but leaving them on a board is just as motivational as a brochure in a high end store.

Breaking down the journey is impactful, adding dates to your goals helps significantly. You will notice that during your moments of self work and professional work you're headed somewhere. The mountain is only there to be conquered, climbed, then taken back down. Could you breathe in the air up at the top forever. It may seem, that you're finding parts of you show up at work, home, or with your friends. Are they different? It's okay for them to be. Each part of you is taking you towards your North Star. No one gets close to understanding your version of the reality you seek. You must be willing to sacrifice, time for pleasure. Find pleasure in your own belonging over fitting in. That's when time is spent best, authentic memories are made. At the top of your mountain, know that only those who wanted you there got you there. Demons spawn along the way, we must be stronger than them.

I keep my vibes bright, sunset hues.
Autobahn mentality straight to you.
Washing out the sands from my ankles,
Making my way out of the depths of the bottomless ocean for you.
I've poured myself into others, I've never held hands the way you know.
I love you.
We hold our happiness together, through every climate any weather.
A soft kiss is what you wished for, a little rumble before noon.
A couple roses in the morning help, only you truly bloom.
Quivering skin, chills in my arms.
My lover is here, pause all the calls.
DND, DND, only room for you & me…
Today.

RESONATE

Suffocation, in my own airspace.
Heaviness, how so? Thin frame everything has been a race.
Redemption, for dollars taken in front of my family.
Questing, for all the gems the weak have left for me.
Drifting, away from the moments of harmony.
Regretfully, I smiled too much and cared so little.
Undoubtedly, I came out to the top and smiled last.
Last.
All of you - Where are you now?
Wandering.
Looking for me?
Each day a coin toss, a mind lost at sea.
Treasure chests filled with gold buried beneath.
I'll never be a swan song, I'm a diver.
Drowning, just enough to feel no oxygen.
Are these mating calls...
Liar. Liar.
I've been blamed, still alive.
I walk amongst you all, don't need you to live.
I'll hold my stories, you won't know what gives.

You may have silenced me,
Yet I do have control of my actions.
I've been told the same words, healed before.
Will again, no mercy my friend.
No worry in my head.
Judgment falls on the shoulders of the dead.
Send the locks to your mind, deadbolts and passcodes now to get in my head.
Who are you to say the journey ends this way.
Silence me again and know I'll bring an army back.
When I find myself in my head -
I'll bury the many who doubted and said I just acted to pretend.
Tearing up their words - living my way instead.

WILLOW

Red lips sent the men downtown,
Uptown they they would only deal blood.
They knew if they heard the horses, bullets would soon arrive too.
For their town was quiet, they laid brick and silvered trinkets.
The boys across the yard would throw rocks, they'd fire back with finger pistols.
You don't feel safe and how could you have known?
You know my train could take you home.
You know there will be a fire, a place to warm your heart, to serve your eyes.
You won't be a passerby no more.
Just a stranger my train brought home.
So what's your name? Are you ashamed?
Of the journey you've had or the one you'll soon embark on.
Don't let the men from the town confuse you, fires burn in all of them.
Lust, broken desires, and misfortune spite them.
Keep walking, keep coming forward.
My hand is here, my tickets in hand.
Let's go home.

Sometimes we paint ourselves in the colors of each other.
Or so we hope.
See I stand with the fog, the gray.
Somewhere lost in the fray.
If I could blend away from the normalcy - I will and I have.
For there are areas in this world where I hide with shoulders shrugged.
I don't wish to die a liar - a deceptive martyr.
I wish for my truths to live clearly - to be like water.
Heavy hands tell me there's power in this world.
Yet I want none of it.
Let me be in between.
Let me be gray.

SO WE ALL FALL DOWN

We've sent our angels into delirium,
They are awake beyond our wildest dreams.
Time is no longer your keeper only the practice of patience.
For life taught you to be proactive,
Reactive.
Active.
Alive.
Remember your past includes the thoughts of yesterday.
Who controlled your smile?
Who tamed your mind and how many miles did you tread towards the cliff.
Are you on the rocky shores claimed as waves mismatching cadence's -
Are you energized by a man's soliloquies.
Do you wish to be happy but sit with depression in your head.
The voice in your head is it really one of a demon.
Pinch yourself it's you and you're welcoming your own obscenities.
What if it's your angels singing the rest of your synapses to sleep.
The struggle is present in us all and yes, the pain is hard to keep
and we all need our own serums for them to leave.
Substance and sustenance.
Mischief and masochism.
Humans.
Managing it all trying to find,
A life that isn't so…
Confined.
Between the nerves, feelings of truth and disbelief.
Afford more hope and love.
Say I love you, to yourself today,
and everyday of the week.
No matter your color or creed.
There's a soul in you, bearing seeds.
For things fall apart &
Our angels don't sleep.

Maybe there's a place where live hearts go to rest,
Just to breakaway for a different set of symphonies.
For change needs to take place, the agony the apathy.
The tragedies and maladies.
Where it will learn again,
How to be honest with itself and mend.
For any reason to see -
A reason to smile in a home, to experience harmony.

I beg of that place.

So where do we send our hearts when home is worse than the doors outside.
Or is it my bed where my heart empties.
Its lullabies have been silenced, for only when I rise -
Will my heart get its energy.
Yet when I rest, it won't so I won't.

RESONATE

As I watch others place bets for things only God and his children go through, I prayed to God this morning asking Him to offer me the strength to bet on myself -
I've longed to rid myself of complacency and its hardships.
I'm searching for the answers only I have to give,
To my being -
For it's my life to live.
Loving myself is a blessing I no longer wish to run from,
As I take apart my faults I wish to remember all the good I have formed.
The praise I hear from others no longer has its power,
I've heard them before -
Yet they're never there during my twilight hours.
My soul is here to stay, no matter who chooses to cheer me on.
I will belong, I will belong -
For myself everyday from here on.

There are no birds in the sky, it's every man for himself.
Forge the right alliance, find the right evac.
Armor your heart for your body will be tested.
Be patient and watch every corner, even for the long distance liars.
We're all soldiers running from gunfire,
You can't scream loud enough - there are bullets of disgrace headed your way.
In the battlefield that is love -
Every bandolier has heartbreak powdered shut.
Remember to fire back -
They're reloading faster than you can figure out where the deathly whispers are coming from.
Close quarters to friendly fire, be careful where you tread and run.
For a damning heartless bloodshed awaits us all.
Find the one to save, the one to save for each other's fate.
Get up, even when you fall.
You owe it to yourself to find the right one.

In his life he made many mistakes. Some more catastrophic than others. Maybe like ordering his eggs sunny side up on overcast days and skipping the butter on the toast just crunching away for the sake of food. He'd smile, but it was as crooked as the table legs barely holding their own weight. The waitress would leave the check without saying thank you for he just pointed at the menu and ordered away. Refused to conversate with anyone. As bitter as the coffee in front of him, he would think to himself maybe she spit in it before giving it him. Wouldn't surprise him, nothing more would that day.

He'd read the paper sitting in the padded chair wondering why the world only talks about the sadness on the front pages and maybe a happy element in the crossword section. A word he'd never seen before broken apart for a new meaning.

As he continued to fill out the puzzle he'd continue to order toast and coffee. Just that. Crunching away at the table where he was then joined by the waitress on her break. He was guessing she was done with his charades act and wanted him to speak to her. Like he would every day except today. She asked him,

"What's the worst thing you've ever done? You don't seem sad, you seem disappointed." He said, "Precisely, I'm disappointed. I prepared my heart for defeat before I gave it a chance to love her. Now she's the one that got away." Her face filled with regret as she gathered herself to walk away saying, "You didn't get her but at least you can eat and breathe the same. Cheer up honey, next round of your day is on me." As she made her way outside for a smoke he'd look into his pockets and rush outside with her. Found his pack and lighter. Carried the light from her to him and they both puffed away. He said, "Love escaped me too many times. I've been trying to remember which time hurt me the most. This time might be the worst." She laughed, "You're never going to find your love without preparing to surpass this moment. No one wants to read 'I've ruined myself' all over your face. How'd ya think I knew right away?"

He continued to take his drags, even let out a few mumbled curse words as she ashed her smoke out. Tied her hair up again and said, "You're more than welcome back inside." He wandered the streets for some time trying to find God shining a light on somebody so he may ask them for answers. That never happened. He'd look to his hands and how they weren't webbed against another, how alone he felt.

He returned to his seat by the window, placed his hands on the coffee mug and found a pen sitting there. Crossing out words on the newspaper trying to make a story out of what's already in print. He found the words of others and made his own.

I don't know where I stand with your heart. Am I at the beginning of loving you or at the finish line.

The article he was scratching words from was about a passionate athlete during their Olympic experience. Except he wasn't standing at a medal ceremony and this finish line he couldn't train for. More toast and more coffee hours went by.

The sunset came out and blanketed the sky in darkness. He felt more at home now than he did in his own. It was the diner where they first met. The first time he said, "I got this one." That wasn't all he wanted to take from that night. To his surprise the same napkin holder she wrote her phone number on turned to the new one he'd use to clean his hands from the crumbs.

It was that chance he never took. The number he never called. The smile he always remembered. The story he forgot to keep writing waiting for her to come back to that diner again. When he stepped away for a few minutes the waitress arrived and read his little blacked out newspaper story. She only had one thing to say in her head, "He only has himself to blame. Taking chances isn't for everyone. Taking them in your head gets you nowhere." She took away his bill and walked away.

He came back to a clean table. The newspaper, mug, plate, and pen were not there anymore but there was a note.

It read, "I usually take tips but this time I'm leaving you one. Call her. Tell her how you feel. I want to see you smile again. Don't come back here without her."

Thank You

The purpose of this book, timeline my life. In a new way. I've learned through thousands of mistakes. I've hidden from this Earth because of it, at least a million times. Have I done more than fumble the keys. Have I been told yes, yet led with my version of no. How have I learned to live in a way that's calm yet at times complacent. There are wolves out there, not like me. I've been questioned and doubted, guided at times only by my beliefs. Held onto the consequences. I've read from many pieces of text. Thousands have poured into my head their love and hate of this world. I've since, along with my own, welcomed their angels and the demons. Empathy is my core. It's who I am, it's where I belong. I've reached a brink before, I reached a breaking point. It set me back, in ways that I've never imagined life to reach. Please remember, there's a hand out there when you need one. There's a car out there with gas to take you away safely to a place your eyes can rest with the galaxy. We're far away. So far away, revolving ourselves with the motions of negatives. We can only go so far, so far until the tears cannot be controlled. You'll ruin yourself thinking of the times, the memories, the many after thoughts. Say all the words you can use to describe ennui. Someone, wants that of you. Someone wishes for you to share. We are not to be kept silent. Our ancestors have fought for our speech. Our kind, our kind has done more to create than I've thought possible. Cartoons and movies offer so much, at a certain age. We'd say, "hah, yeah right." 15 years later, "it happened, they were right." I chose to stay to see what we all can do together, in return my soul rejoiced.

I've chosen to tell my life in these pages. I'm only trying to share so that those after me can see this and think: have I been there? Could that be me? What is being told through these pages? How can I keep them inside their mind. Let them drip into every word. Stare at times, focus them, observe. I hope I've resonated with you in some way. Take care and remember to choose yourself over your ego. Remember our greatest blessing was another's hope.

It's been a pleasure,
Aarav Chopra

"And I said what I felt, no re-write." - Childish Gambino

Help is available
Speak with someone today

National Suicide Prevention Lifeline
Hours: Available 24 hours.
1-800-273-8255

RESONATE

Aarav Chopra

www.ingramcontent.com/pod-product-compliance
Lightning Source LLC
Chambersburg PA
CBHW021949290426
44108CB00012B/998